A Curious Student's Guide to the Book of Deuteronomy

A Curious Student's Guide to the Book of Deuteronomy

Enduring Life Lessons for the Twenty-First Century

REUVEN TRAVIS

WIPF & STOCK · Eugene, Oregon

A CURIOUS STUDENT'S GUIDE TO THE BOOK OF DEUTERONOMY
Enduring Life Lessons for the Twenty-First Century

Copyright © 2022 Reuven Travis. All rights reserved. Except for brief quotations in critical publications or reviews, no part of this book may be reproduced in any manner without prior written permission from the publisher. Write: Permissions, Wipf and Stock Publishers, 199 W. 8th Ave., Suite 3, Eugene, OR 97401.

Wipf & Stock
An Imprint of Wipf and Stock Publishers
199 W. 8th Ave., Suite 3
Eugene, OR 97401

www.wipfandstock.com

PAPERBACK ISBN: 978-1-6667-3758-5
HARDCOVER ISBN: 978-1-6667-9717-6
EBOOK ISBN: 978-1-6667-9718-3

05/31/22

Original illustrations by Eli Portman.

I think, at a child's birth, if a mother could ask a fairy godmother to endow it with the most useful gift, that gift would be curiosity.
—ELEANOR ROOSEVELT

Contents

Acknowledgements | ix
Preface for Parents and Educators | xi
A Listing of the Commandments in Deuteronomy | xxiii

Devarim
    Part One: Why is This Book Different
        From All Other Books? | 1
    Part Two: The Farewell Begins | 6
Va'etchanan | 19
Eikev | 33
Re'eh | 41
Shoftim | 51
Ki Teitzei | 59
Ki Tavo | 65
Nitzavim | 71
Vayelech | 83
Haazinu | 91
V'Zot HaBeracha | 99

Postscript | 109
About the Author | 113

Acknowledgements

My dad was seventy-four when he died in 2006, too young in absolute terms, but given his underlying health issues, perhaps we were fortunate to have him with us for that long.

I often think of my dad, especially at lifecycle or milestone events, such as the wedding of a child, the birth of a grandchild, or even the publication of this book, which marks the conclusion of my Curious Student's Guide series.

My dad would have gotten great pleasure from these events and the many things he missed in the years since his passing. He did not see his grandchildren grow into remarkable human beings, each enjoying much success in his or her chosen profession. He did not meet the fine young men my daughters married or experience the loving homes they have created. He would never have understood my son's success in trading crypto currencies (I certainly don't), nonetheless, he would have been proud. He never experienced the special hugs and kisses that only a great-grandchild can give.

And he never read a single book I've published.

My writing career, such as it is, pales in comparison to these family-related events. I say that with no hesitation, and Dad would have agreed. Family was first and foremost to him, and it is the most important life lesson he ever imparted to me.

That said, Dad would have taken special joy from this Curious Student's Guide series. He often (and lovingly) would tease

Acknowledgements

me and ask when I was finally going to become a college professor. That's how he imagined me in the later years of his life. I have earned neither a title nor tenure by publishing this series, but I like to think it would have been close enough for my dad.

Rabbi Reuven Travis

Preface for Parents and Educators

The opening of the book of Deuteronomy seems quite unambiguous about its authorship, as well as the when's and the where's of its composition.

> These are the words that Moses addressed to all Israel on the other side of the Jordan.—Through the wilderness, in the Arabah near Suph, between Paran and Tophel, Laban, Hazeroth, and Di-zahab, it is eleven days from Horeb to Kadesh-barnea by the Mount Seir route.—It was in the fortieth year, on the first day of the eleventh month, that Moses addressed the Israelites in accordance with the instructions that the LORD had given him for them, after he had defeated Sihon king of the Amorites, who dwelt in Heshbon, and King Og of Bashan, who dwelt at Ashtaroth [and] Edrei. (Deuteronomy 1:1–4)

Deuteronomy is, all agree, Moses's book. It is his farewell address, delivered during the seven weeks leading up to his death and the Jewish people's entry into the land of Canaan under Joshua's leadership. And because it is Moses's book, Deuteronomy's tone, linguistic structure, and content, all differ greatly from the other four books of the Torah. To truly understand Deuteronomy, one must understand the history of the book, and that requires an understanding of a bit of Jewish history.

The final decades of the first temple era were tumultuous years. A wicked king would rule, only to be succeeded by a

Preface for Parents and Educators

righteous king, who in turn was succeeded by yet another wicked and ineffectual king. Without question, the worst of these kings was Manasseh.

Manasseh, the only son of the righteous Hezekiah, became king at an age of 12. He reigned for fifty-five years, the longest reign in the history of the monarchy of Judah.[1] Manasseh is harshly criticized in the rabbinic tradition for his re-institution of pagan worship and his reversal of the religious reforms made by his father Hezekiah. Here is how Joseph Herman Hertz, Chief Rabbi of the United Kingdom from 1913 until 1946, described the reign of Manasseh:

> He nearly succeeded in uprooting True Religion in Israel and flooded the land with obscene and gruesome idolatries. The Temple itself did not escape profanation: the sacred Altar was desecrated; the Ark itself was removed from out of the Holy of Holies; and new altars were erected for various weird cults. His years were one long Reign of Terror to the loyal minority who attempted to withstand the tide of religious barbarism.[2]

In the eyes of the rabbis, Manasseh was the embodiment of wickedness. Notwithstanding the fact that he repented late in life and reversed his previous actions. (2 Kings 21:2–16; 2 Chronicles 33:2–19), the aftereffects of Manasseh's wickedness would reverberate throughout the years leading up to the destruction of the first temple.

Things did not improve after the death of Manasseh, who was succeeded by his son Amon. Amon was twenty-two when he ascended to the throne and reigned for only two years.[3] Sadly, Amon continued his father's practice of idolatry, going so far as to set up the pagan images as his father had done. The prophet Zephaniah describes Amon's reign as one of moral depravity.[4] Amon, who was

---

1. 2 Kings 21:1; 2 Chronicles 33:1.
2. Joseph Herman Hertz, "Deuteronomy: Its Antiquity and Mosaic Authorship," in *The Pentateuch and the Haftorahs*, ed. Dr. J. H. Hertz (London: Soncino Press, 1960), 937.
3. 2 Kings 21:18–19.
4. Zephaniah 1:4; also 3:4, and 11.

assassinated by his servants, was succeeded by his son Josiah, who was eight years old.[5]

It is during the reign of Josiah that the history of the book of Deuteronomy takes an interesting twist.

Because he was a child when he inherited the throne, Josiah was guided by a group of pious and loyal supporters, including the High Priest Hilkiah and his son Jeremiah, the royal scribe Shaphan and his son Ahikam, and the royal chamberlain Shallum and his wife the prophetess Huldah. Their influence on the young king would soon become apparent.

Eight years after his formal installation, Josiah began to assert his royal authority. He wished to change the direction of his kingdom, but he moved cautiously against the nobility who, under Manasseh and Amon, had garnered great power and who were disinclined to change the status quo, either religiously or secularly. Only after four years could Josiah push these men aside and surround himself with responsible, God-fearing advisors.

Like his great-grandfather Hezekiah, Josiah sought God and purged the land of all forms of idolatry. As 2 Kings tells us, "He did what was pleasing to the LORD and he followed all the ways of his ancestor David; he did not deviate to the right or to the left."[6] This culminated when, in the eighteenth year of his rule, Josiah announced a plan to renovate the temple. While the repairs were being made, the High Priest Hilkiah found an ancient scroll[7]: one thought to be a Torah scroll that Moses himself wrote.[8] Hilkiah gave it to Shaphan to bring it to the king's attention. The king

---

5. 2 Kings 22:1.
6. 2 Kings 22:2.
7. Hertz notes that in the Ancient Near East, books of religious law and sacred documents were deposited in temples during their construction and were often "discovered" when these building were renovated. Hertz, "Deuteronomy: Its Antiquity and Mosaic Authorship," 937.
8. The rabbinic tradition subscribes to the belief that, before his death, Moses wrote thirteen Torah scrolls. Twelve of these were given to the twelve tribes. The thirteenth was placed in the Ark of the Covenant. For reasons left unstated in the text, Hilkiah believes that this long-hidden scroll was one of these thirteen.

commanded him to read from it. The biblical narrative does not name which passages from this Torah scroll were read to the king, but the rabbinic tradition states that Hilkiah read the passage where Moses warns that if the Jewish people fail to follow God's ways they will be heavily punished.

> Take care not to be lured away to serve other gods and bow to them. For the LORD's anger will flare up against you, and He will shut up the skies so that there will be no rain and the ground will not yield its produce; and you will soon perish from the good land that the LORD is assigning to you.[9]

Apparently, it had been many years since the people and their leaders studied Deuteronomy. When Josiah heard the terrible prophecies set forth in that book, he was shaken to his core. He realized the depths to which the people had sunk during the reigns of his father and grandfather because of their immorality and idolatry, and he was fearful of the looming consequences of the people's sinful actions. Josiah rent his clothes and sent a delegation headed by Hilkiah to consult the prophetess Huldah. Namely, he wished to know what punishments were in store for the people and whether or not they could be averted.

After hearing Huldah's message,[10] Josiah understood that the people needed to hear the long-lost words of Deuteronomy and embark on a path of repentance. As II Kings describes the scene,

> The king went up to the House of the LORD, together with all the men of Judah and all the inhabitants of Jerusalem, and the priests and prophets—all the people, young and old. And he read to them the entire text of the covenant scroll which had been found in the House of the LORD. The king stood by the pillar and solemnized the covenant before the LORD: that they would follow the LORD and observe His commandments, His injunctions, and His laws with all their heart and soul; that they would fulfill all the terms of this covenant as

---

9. Deuteronomy 11: 16–17.
10. 2 Kings 22:15–20.

inscribed upon the scroll. And all the people entered into the covenant.[11]

The words Josiah shared with the people (and that the people took upon themselves to follow) may have been new to them, but they were *not* new. In the traditional Jewish perspective, Deuteronomy is an ancient text that Moses himself authored. The thought is, however, that it had been lost until Josiah's time.

Many secular scholars dismiss this account.

As early as the sixteenth century, English deists were putting forward the notion that Deuteronomy was a forgery.[12] However, it was towards the end of the eighteenth century that scholars began to more forcefully question the origins and authorship of Deuteronomy. No one was more influential in this new movement than Johann Salomo Semler.[13] Semler maintained that the idea of divine inspiration and Mosaic authorship of Deuteronomy were matters of faith, and as such, "as little provable as . . . demonstrable."[14] Semler's argument, in simplest terms, was this: the various books of the Bible were and ought to be thought of as books written by humans and should thus be read and studied as such. On Semler's influence, Stefan Schreiner has written that "with this distinction between the divine content of the Word on the one hand and this Word given a human shape by man on the other, [Semler] had in principle paved the way for a new form of Bible study."[15]

The history of this movement, as it evolved and was guided by the likes of Eduard Reuss (1804–1891), Karl Heinrich Graf (1815–1896), Hermann Hupfeld (1796–1866), and Julius Wellhausen (1844–1914), among others, is beyond the scope of this brief introduction. Suffice it to say that the advent of this new

---

11. 2 Kings 23:2–3.

12. Hertz, 938.

13. Stefan Schreiner, "Protestant Bible Study and the Jewish Response in the 19th and 20th Centuries," *Jewish Studies Quarterly* 10, no. 2 (2003): 144.

14. Schreiner, 144.

15. Schreiner, 144.

school of biblical criticism gave rise to a number of theories regarding Deuteronomy.[16]

The first question to be addressed by these theories was, who wrote the book and when? All biblical critics agree that the book of Deuteronomy was not written by Moses but by some unknown author or authors. When it was written is another matter altogether. While many date the book to the reign of King Josiah (or shortly before that reign), some critics say that Hilkiah himself was the author of the book. Others believe the book was written before Josiah's time, perhaps as early as the time of Manasseh or even the days of his maternal grandfather Isaiah.[17]

These theories must also explain why there was a need to craft a book such as Deuteronomy. An answer often given is that "its author or authors hoped by means of it to promote a religious Reformation, a return to the true God, in Israel."[18] This answer seems quite consistent with the account of Deuteronomy's "discovery" (set forth in 2 Kings) that we have already discussed.

Semler, as we have seen, felt that one's views on Deuteronomy must inevitably be shaped by one's faith. That may no longer be true, and here's why. Admittedly, there are people of faith—Jews, Christians, or Muslims—who reject biblical criticism out of hand. Recognizing it and accepting it would, in their minds, undermine the divine nature of the Bible. Nonetheless, there increasingly are others

---

16. Biblical criticism is best thought of as the use of critical analysis to understand and explain the Bible. During the eighteenth century, it focused on historical-biblical criticism, with the view that the reconstruction of historical events depicted in the biblical texts, as well as the history of how the texts themselves developed, would lead to a correct understanding of the Bible itself. In the late twentieth and early twenty-first century, biblical criticism was evolving, as it was increasingly influenced by a wide range of additional academic disciplines and theoretical perspectives. including Near Eastern studies, psychology, cultural anthropology, and sociology. The field continues to advance, as post-modernism and post-critical interpretation have begun to question whether biblical criticism had a role and function at all.

17. A.P. Gold-Levin, "Deuteronomy—Whence and Why? A Study in Scripture Criticism and Hebrew Psychology," *The Evangelical Quarterly* 1 (1929): 33.

18. Gold-Levin, 33.

Preface for Parents and Educators

who recognize the divine in the Bible and its continued relevance to our lives regardless of who wrote it when. For these individuals, biblical criticism does not challenge their faith. It enhances it.[19]

How you as a parent relate to this issue is between you and your God (with perhaps some guidance from your clergy). But it is not a topic that ought to be discussed or even broached with young students. If adults struggle with this concept, then it is reasonable to believe that it is just too complex and abstract for young minds to fully grapple with. What matters when teaching Torah to your children or to your younger students is the life lessons you can help them discover as they read through Deuteronomy (with your help, of course). And that is what this book is all about.

In addition to these debates about the authorship of Deuteronomy, there is much discussion among scholars and rabbis about the nature of the book itself. One of the Hebrew names for Deuteronomy is *Mishneh Torah*, which means "Repetition of the Torah."[20] This name is reflective of the idea that Moses, in Deuteronomy, repeats and reteaches many of the laws he shared with the Jewish people during their forty years in the Sinai wilderness. He apparently feels compelled to do this so that the generation raised in the wilderness will be better prepared to enter and conquer the land of Canaan while remaining faithful servants to their God. Thus, he retells to this younger generation the wonders of the face-to-face encounter the people had with God at Mount Sinai and reteaches

---

19. There are serious Orthodox Jewish scholars and rabbis who have written extensively on how to reconcile biblical criticism with one's belief in God and the divinity of the Bible. See, for example, Dr. Rabbi Zev Farber's "Can Orthodox Education Survive Biblical Criticism?" (https://www.thetorah.com/article/can-orthodox-education-survive-biblical-criticism). See also Dr. Rabbi Joshua Berman's recent book entitled *Ani Maamin: Biblical Criticism, Historical Truth, and the Thirteen Principles of Faith* (Jerusalem: Maggid Books, 2020). Neither of these authors shies away from the difficult questions that biblical criticism can pose about the structure of Torah and the inconsistencies sometimes found therein.

20. This term, *Mishneh Torah*, is found in Deuteronomy 17:17, which describes the obligation of the king of Israel to have a Torah scroll with him at all times: "When he is seated on his royal throne, he shall have a copy of this Teaching (*Mishneh Torah*) written for him on a scroll by the levitical priests."

PREFACE FOR PARENTS AND EDUCATORS

them the Ten Commandments.[21] He reviews with them the story of the spies and the terrible outcome that resulted from their parents believing the evil report of the spies, in the hope that those about to enter the land of Israel would not repeat the mistakes of the previous generation. But Moses skips the story of the golden calf, for he is convinced that this generation will not succumb to the temptations of idolatry.

All this is true, but this approach overlooks a fundamental fact about Deuteronomy: that it is not merely a "Repetition of the Torah." In reality, it contains more than seventy commandments found nowhere else in the Torah. (A list of these commandments can be found at the end of this introduction.) Most of these pertain to the land of Israel and the obligations incumbent upon those who dwell in the land. However, some very basic commandments (such as the requirement to wear fringes on four-cornered garments, the laws of the three pilgrimage festivals, and the dietary laws) are in fact repeated in Deuteronomy. This prompted Rabbi Samson Raphael Hirsch[22] to comment, "To appreciate the tendency of this fifth book one must find out why those new laws were reserved to be given only here at the end, and why, out of the whole Torah which Moses repeated to the people, just those were again picked out to be again fixed in the written text."[23]

Making sure that young students grasp this point—that there is more to Deuteronomy than a repetition of stories and laws from the other four books of the Torah—is critical to their understanding of Deuteronomy.

---

21. As discussed in *A Curious Guide to the Book of Exodus,* they are more correctly called "the Ten Utterances" because, as a correct reading of the Hebrew text reveals, these ten utterances contain only nine commandments.

22. Rabbi Samson Raphael Hirsch, who lived in Germany during the 1800s, did much in his lifetime to preserve traditional Judaism in the face of the rise of Reform Judaism in Germany. He is perhaps best known as the intellectual founder of the *Torah im Derech Eretz* school of contemporary Orthodox Judaism (sometimes termed neo-Orthodoxy).

23. Samson Raphael Hirsch, *The Pentateuch, Vol. V, Deuteronomy* (London: Judaica Press, 1982), 3.

Preface for Parents and Educators

With this background, we can now turn to a few more observations that should help maximize the utility of this book as you share it with your children and students.

A significant challenge in teaching children the books of the Torah is differentiating between the text itself and the accompanying biblical exegesis. This is particularly tricky in Jewish homes and schools where adults often turn to midrash (a form of biblical exegesis developed and employed by ancient Judaic authorities) as a tool for helping children better understand the biblical narrative. Midrash provides us with important insights into and backstories to the text, but students should never conflate it with the Bible itself. The biblical text is the text; midrash is commentary on the text.

When using midrash to make the text more easily understood (whether in the classroom or at home interacting with my own children), I have always been guided by the approach of Rabbi Moshe ben Nachman (also known as Nachmanides and also by the acronym Ramban), the great biblical commentator from the 1200s. In his famous disputation with the apostate Jew Pablo Christiani, Ramban made this observation:

> We possess three genres of literature. The first is the Bible or Tanakh, and all of us believe in its words with a complete trust. The second is the Talmud, and it is an exposition of the commandments of the Torah, for the Torah contains 613 commandments. Not a single one of them is left unexplained by the Talmud. We believe in the Talmud with respect to its exposition of the commandments. The third type of book that we possess is the Midrash, and it is like sermons. . . . Concerning this collection, for one who believes it, good. For one who does not believe it, there is no harm.[24]

I have never been one to insist that students see midrashic expositions as accurate historical accounts, nor have I framed midrashic stories as mere parables. How a student chooses to see this literature is up to him or her. But what cannot be ignored or diminished are the important lessons midrash offers us. It is equally

---

24. Ramban (Nahmanides), *The Disputation at Barcelona*, paragraph 39.

Preface for Parents and Educators

critical that, when learning these stories, students recognize them as midrash and understand that they are not found in the text of the Torah itself. (Throughout this book, when midrash is used to explain the text, it will be identified as such, or it will be referred to as "the rabbinic tradition.")

In addition to understanding how and when midrash is used in this book, readers should also be familiar with the approach I employ for presenting and examining the central stories of Deuteronomy. In brief, I have opted not to use the system of chapters and verse numbers most students of the Bible are acquainted with. This division was first made in the Latin Bible in the thirteenth century, most likely by Stephen Langston.[25] Langston's system was employed in the concordances of the Vulgate, and this in turn gave Rabbi Isaac Nathan[26] the idea for the first Hebrew concordance. The citations in this concordance first give the number of the Vulgate chapter and then give the number of the masoretic[27] verse chapter, which remains to this day the standard format of the printed Hebrew Bible.

However, the printed format of the Hebrew Bible is not the one used for ritual purposes. As part of Jewish prayer services on the Sabbath, different portions of the Torah are read each week.[28] These readings are commonly referred to as the weekly *parasha* or

---

25. Stephen Langton was an English cardinal of the Roman Catholic Church and Archbishop of Canterbury from 1207 to his death, in 1228. The dispute between King John of England and Pope Innocent III over his election as archbishop was a major factor in the crisis that produced the Magna Carta in 1215.

26. Rabbi Isaac Nathan ben Kalonymus was a French Jewish philosopher who lived in the fourteenth and fifteenth centuries. In the introduction to his concordance, Rabbi Isaac wrote that he was completely ignorant of the Bible until his fifteenth year. Prior to that time, his studies had been restricted to the Talmud and religious philosophy.

27. In rabbinic Judaism, the Masoretic Text is the authoritative Hebrew and Aramaic text of the Bible. It was copied, edited, and distributed primarily by a group of Jews known as the Masoretes between the seventh and tenth centuries CE.

28. There are fifty-four such weekly portions, which means that a double portion is read on some weeks.

Preface for Parents and Educators

sedra. The starting and ending points of each parasha have nothing to do with Langston's system for organizing the Bible. Rather, they reflect the long-standing masoretic tradition.

Given my background and training as an Orthodox rabbi and Jewish educator, it made sense for me to organize this book according to these weekly parashas. It is a system I know well and am comfortable with. More importantly, these weekly readings, in my opinion, present a more logical flow for the major themes and stories of Deuteronomy than do the chapter and verse numbers in common usage.[29]

Each chapter of this book will open with a brief overview and synopsis of the weekly Torah reading. This will be followed by a section I have titled "Life Lessons from This Week's Reading," which has the goal of helping young students think more deeply about the text read each week, as opposed to merely memorizing certain incidents from the narrative. Finally, there will be questions for students to think about as they begin to make the lessons from each week's reading their own.

To help parents and educators contextualize what I think of as the "big picture" questions about Deuteronomy, I have also included a chapter that discusses how and why Deuteronomy differs from the other books of the Torah.

All translations of biblical verses in this book are from *Tanakh: A New Translation of the Holy Scriptures according to the Traditional Hebrew Text* unless otherwise indicated.[30] This translation is available in the public domain and with a free public license thanks to Sefaria (www.sefaria.org), a nonprofit organization that, in its own words, is dedicated to assembling "a free, living library of Jewish texts."

---

29. Indeed, there are many chapter breaks that interrupt the logical flow of the narrative that the masoretic tradition avoids. See, for example, the end of chapter forty-three and the beginning of chapter forty-four. This is clearly a single narrative—one we will discuss in great detail later in this book—and most modern editors would be confounded by the insertion of a new chapter here.

30. *Tanakh: A New Translation of the Holy Scriptures according to the Traditional Hebrew Text* (Philadelphia: Jewish Publication Society, 1985).

A Listing of the Commandments in Deuteronomy

As Rabbi Samson Raphael Hirsch notes, of the over 100 commandments found in Deuteronomy, more than seventy are completely new and are not found in the other four books of the Torah. A partial listing includes:

1. The belief in one God.
2. Prohibition against intermarriage.
3. Prohibition against deriving any benefit from items associated with idol worship.
4. Obligation to bless God after eating a meal.
5. Obeying the commands of God.
6. The blessings and curses to be recited by the tribe of Levi to the people while they stand on Mount Gerizim and Mount Eival.
7. You should not do thusly to your God lest you should come to sin.
8. Prohibition against building private altars.
9. Prohibition against eating sacrificial foods (e.g., those involving tithes, vows, or dedications) in a private domain.
10. Laws involving the kosher slaughtering of animals for food consumption.

A Listing of the Commandments in Deuteronomy

11. Tithes for the poor.
12. Command to offer the blood with the meat of a sacrifice.
13. Do not add to or modify the commandments of the Torah.
14. Laws involving a false prophet.
15. Free-will offering brought by the individual during Shavuot.
16. Laws involving a city under siege by a Jewish army.
17. Laws proscribing how and where one may cut his beard.
18. Forgiving debts every seven years.
19. Charity
20. Establishing a Supreme Court.
21. Prohibition against trees worshipped as idols being near an altar of God.
22. Laws pertaining to an individual who worships idols.
23. Laws involving giving testimony.
24. Laws involving the king.
25. Returning the spoils of war.
26. Giving the priests the first fleecings of the sheep.
27. Establishing shifts of priests to work in the temple.
28. Obeying a true prophet.
29. Prohibition against moving the marker which delineates another's property.
30. Laws involving false witnesses.
31. Obligation to offer peace terms in time of war.
32. Prohibition against being wasteful.
33. Laws involving an unsolved murder.
34. Laws pertaining to a non-Jewish captive taken in time of war.
35. Inheritance laws of the first-born son.
36. The "Rebellious Son."

A Listing of the Commandments in Deuteronomy

37. Do not allow the body of a person executed by hanging to remain dangling from the tree.
38. Prohibition against cross-dressing.
39. Sending away the mother bird before taking her young.
40. The obligation to build a parapet on a roof.
41. Not plowing with an ox and donkey together.
42. Prohibition against gossiping.
43. Prohibitions regarding another man's wife.
44. The betrothed maiden.
45. Laws involving rape.
46. Prohibition against marrying the wife of your father.
47. Laws involving a man with crushed testicles.
48. Laws involving illegitimate children.
49. Prohibition against allowing men of Amon and Moav marry into the Jewish nation.
50. Prohibition against "despising" the Edomite.
51. Prohibition against "despising" the Egyptian.
52. The army camp.
53. Prohibition against use of prostitutes' fees for matters involving the temple.
54. Prohibition against use of "the price of a dog" for matters involving the temple.
55. Laws involving what workers in a vineyard may eat from the vineyard.
56. Divorce
57. Laws involving remarrying one's spouse after a divorce.
58. Allowing a man to be exempt from military service during his first year of marriage.
59. Allowing a man to be exempt from military service during his first year in a new home.

A Listing of the Commandments in Deuteronomy

60. Prohibition against relatives testifying against relatives.
61. Flogging
62. Prohibition against muzzling an ox while it is treading grain.
63. Levirate marriage.
64. Remembering Amalek.
65. The "First Fruits."
66. Declaration for removing tithes.
67. Writing the Torah on large, plastered stone when crossing the Jordan to enter the land of Israel.
68. Obligation to assembly the people every seven years during Sukkot to hear the words of the Torah.
69. Obligation to write a Torah scroll.

Devarim

(Deuteronomy 1:1—3:22)

Part One: Why is This Book Different From All Other Books?

One of the most common phrases in the Torah is "And the LORD spoke to Moses saying." So many of the Torah's commandments are introduced in this way. These words represent God speaking to Moses and instructing him what to repeat to or teach the Jewish people. Yet, this phrase is not found at all in Deuteronomy, and this helps explain why this book is so very different from the other books of the Torah. You see, Deuteronomy is Moses's book. It is the record of Moses's final speech to the Jewish people before his death. But this leads us to ask a very basic and very fundamental question. Why are the words of man, even a man as great as Moses, part of God's holy Torah?

Strange as it may seem, this question only occurred to me when I started working on this book. Such an obvious question, and yet, I never stopped to ask why Deuteronomy is part of the Torah. I just took for granted that it has always been part of the Torah. And now, having asked the question, I must confess that I have yet to find a good answer.

Not having a good answer may be disappointing, but it is not concerning. One of the themes I have returned to throughout this Curious Student's Guide series is the importance of asking questions. Asking questions shows that we're interested in what we're studying. Questions reflect deep thinking on a subject and demonstrate that we desire to know more. Just coming up with and asking good questions is always worthwhile, even if or when those questions remain unanswered.

So, rather than answer the question of why Deuteronomy is part of the Torah, let's step back and try to explain why this is such an important question.

You may recall that the book of Numbers tells us about the forty years the Jews wandered through the Sinai wilderness on their way to Canaan: the land God promised to the descendants of Abraham, Isaac, and Jacob. One of the most important and confusing stories in Numbers takes place near the end of the Jew's travels through the wilderness. In the story, as the Jews are moving closer and closer to Canaan, Moses's sister Miriam dies. This is a major turning point because while Miriam is alive, a well miraculously follows the Jews, providing them water. After Miriam dies, the well disappears. Understandably, the people are scared, and they are on the verge of panic. What will they drink? Where will they find water?

The people of course turn to Moses for answers, and he in turn turns to God. God tells Moses to go to the Tabernacle (*mishkan* in Hebrew) which is located in the center of the camp. There he is to enter the Holy of Holies, take his staff from the ark where it has been hidden away for many years, and then go to a rock God will show him. God tells Moses to stand in front of the rock and speak to it. It will provide all the water the people need.

Moses does as he is told. He takes his staff and stands before the rock. However, it is at this point that something unexpected happens. Moses does not speak to the rock. He hits the rock. Not once, but twice. And he gets very angry with the people and calls them rebels. In His great mercy, God makes water flow from the rock even though Moses did not do as he was told. God is upset with Moses though. So upset that He tells Moses he will not be allowed to lead the people into Canaan. He will instead die in the wilderness and never set foot in the promised land.

It's such a strange story. To this day, rabbis and scholars debate which of Moses's actions upset God. Was it because he hit the rock instead of speaking to it? Was it because he hit the rock two times? (Once would have been enough to produce the miracle.) Was it because he was angry with the people when God Himself was not? (Who could be angry with people who are scared about being in a desert with nothing to drink?)

The truth is, we don't know why God was so upset, only that He was very upset. And the story gets stranger still.

We might have thought that Moses would die a quiet, private death (no farewell parties and no farewell speeches) as did his siblings Aaron and Miriam.[1] But God is merciful and thus allows Moses to speak to the people one last time before his death. And what a speech! Moses speaks not for an hour or two, not even for a day or two. God allows Moses to speak for weeks and weeks. In his speech, Moses reviews the Jews' journeys through the Sinai wilderness to help the people avoid repeating mistakes they made along the way once they enter Canaan. He reteaches hundreds of commandments that he had taught the people over the past forty years. He also introduces and teaches new laws and commandments that only apply to the land of Israel and are only observed when the people are living in Israel.

Had God stopped here, *dayeinu*, it would have been enough. It would have been a great final gift to a great man who had served God faithfully all his life. But God's mercy is beyond the ability of people to understand. He grants Moses an even greater gift. God includes Moses's farewell address to the Jewish people in the Torah.

---

1. Chapter twenty of the book of Numbers (verses 24–29) provides us with a simple description of Aaron's death: "Let Aaron be gathered to his kin: he is not to enter the land that I have assigned to the Israelite people, because you disobeyed my command about the Waters of Meribah. Take Aaron and his son Eleazar and bring them up on Mount Hor. Strip Aaron of his vestments and put them on his son Eleazar. There Aaron shall be gathered into the dead. Moses did as the LORD had commanded. They ascended Mount Hor in the sight of the whole community. Moses stripped Aaron of his vestments and put them on his son Eleazar, and Aaron died there on the summit of the mountain. When Moses and Eleazar came down from the mountain, the whole community knew that Aaron had breathed his last. All the house of Israel bewailed Aaron thirty days."

The words of a man, even one as great as Moses, included in God's holy book? Amazing! Remarkable! And quite inexplicable!

Now, perhaps the importance of the question—why include Moses's speech (as the book of Deuteronomy) in the Torah?—is clear. And now, perhaps you can also understand why I've yet to find an answer.

Deuteronomy—as the words of man—certainly explains why it is so different from the rest of the Torah. However, there are a few more differences you should be aware of that help make Deuteronomy a unique book.

Let's start with the name of the book itself.

The English names of the books of the Torah are not English words at all. They were first used in a Greek translation of the Torah that was written more than two thousand years ago.[2] Deuteronomy comes from a Greek word that many think means "second law" or "repeated law." Others believe "copy" or "repetition" more accurately reflect its meaning. This Greek title echoes a nickname given over the centuries for this book by the rabbis, *Mishneh Torah*, which, like the Greek, means "second law" or "repeated law."

Both names, Deuteronomy and *Mishneh Torah*, are a bit misleading. People often think that Deuteronomy contains no new commandments because Moses, in his farewell speech, simply reviews what he has been teaching the people for forty years. It is certainly true that some very basic commandments are repeated in Deuteronomy. However, Deuteronomy also contains more than seventy commandments found nowhere else in the Torah.

There is one other thing that sets Deuteronomy apart from the other books of the Torah. The Talmudic sages taught that Moses wrote thirteen Torah scrolls before he died.[3] According to this tradition, Moses gave a scroll to each of the twelve tribes and placed a thirteenth in the Ark of the Covenant (along with the tablets he brought down from Mount Sinai). So far, so good. However,

---

2. This translation, known as the Septuagint, is believed to have been written from the third through the first centuries BCE.

3. *Devarim Rabba* 9:9.

a question arises about who wrote the final eight verses of the book of Devarim. Here are the verses:

> So Moses the servant of the LORD died there, in the land of Moab, at the command of the LORD. He buried him in the valley in the land of Moab, near Beth-peor; and no one knows his burial place to this day. Moses was a hundred and twenty years old when he died; his eyes were undimmed and his vigor unabated. And the Israelites bewailed Moses in the steppes of Moab for thirty days. The period of wailing and mourning for Moses came to an end. Now Joshua son of Nun was filled with the spirit of wisdom because Moses had laid his hands upon him; and the Israelites heeded him, doing as the LORD had commanded Moses. Never again did there arise in Israel a prophet like Moses—whom the LORD singled out, face to face, for the various signs and portents that the LORD sent him to display in the land of Egypt, against Pharaoh and all his courtiers and his whole country, and for all the great might and awesome power that Moses displayed before all Israel.

The Talmudic rabbis debate whether Moses actually wrote these verses because they describe his death, his burial, and the mourning period the Jewish people observed for him. One view is that Moses wrote the words describing his own death (with tears streaming down his face) as they were dictated by God. The second view says that Joshua added these verses to the written Torah scrolls at the command of God after the death of Moses.[4]

No matter which of these two opinions makes more sense to you, and no matter how much of Deuteronomy is a repetition of "old" commandments verses the teaching of "new" ones, one thing is clear. A person cannot fully study and fully understand the Torah without carefully studying this complex and unique book.

Enough with the teasers. Let's get started!

---

4. Talmud Bavli Menachot 30a, Gittin 60a.

Devarim

(Deuteronomy 1:1—3:22)

Part Two: The Farewell Begins

Summary of This Week's Reading

Deuteronomy, which is all about Moses's farewell address to the Jewish people, begins five weeks before his death, and this first reading sets the tone for the entire book. Here Moses looks back and retells stories from the wanderings of the Jews in the wilderness. He uses these stories to teach people about things they should do (or not do!) once they enter Canaan. Moses also looks ahead. When he does, he gives very specific instructions about their entry into and conquest of the land of Canaan. We will encounter this pattern throughout our study of Deuteronomy.

If you look carefully at the beginning of our reading, you will see that Moses does not begin his speech (and thus the book of Deuteronomy) with a story. Rather, he starts by naming the date and exact place where he is giving his speech. At first glance, this seems a bit unusual. Does it really matter where and when he gave this speech? As we will see shortly, this introduction is actually a code Moses uses to soften his criticism of the Jewish people.

Now, on to the stories we find in this week's reading.

The first story takes places thirty-nine years earlier, before the Jewish people left Mount Sinai (at God's command) to continue their journey to Canaan. At that time, Moses came to realize that he could not single-handedly hear all the questions of the people and give decisions on all their legal issues. Moses decides to appoint a series of

Devarim (Deuteronomy 1:1—3:22)

judges to help him hear and decide the hundreds of cases brought to him each day. The people see what a wise decision this was, and they embrace it. Moses reminds them how, at that time, he taught them the importance of having honest and fair judges.

Moses continues and describes how the Jews traveled through the desert and quickly reached Kadesh Barnea, on the southern border of Canaan. It seemed, at least back then, that the conquest of Canaan was about to begin. However, the people came to Moses and insisted that spies be sent ahead to scout out the land. (Having read the book of Numbers, we know how badly that turned out!) Moses reviews the whole story in detail because, having listened to the false reports of the spies, the Jews were not allowed to enter Canaan. They instead spent a total of forty years wandering in the Sinai wilderness.

It makes great sense for Moses to retell this story. The Jewish people are again at the border of Canaan and are again getting ready to enter the land. Under Joshua's leadership (after the death of Moses), spies are again sent ahead, but Joshua and the people remember Moses's words of warning, and that story (as told in the second chapter of the book of Joshua) has a happier ending.

Moses continues with his story: After the people accepted the false report of the spies, God told the Jews to turn around and head back to the desert. Only now did the people understand what a big mistake they had made. Some of them decided to try and correct their mistake. They ignored God's command and headed towards Canaan, intent on entering and conquering the land. As Moses reminds them, he plead with them not to ignore God's command. By doing so, God would remove His divine protection from them. They ignored both God and Moses and were immediately attacked and massacred by the Emorites. Only then did the people listen to the word of God and head back to the Sinai Desert.

Time for a new story.

In this one, Moses fast-forwards thirty-eight years. By this time, all the men twenty years and older who had left Egypt had died. It is their children who were ready to enter Canaan. But, as Moses reminds them, God gave them very clear rules for conquering the land. God told the Jews that the lands of three nations—Seir (Edom), Moab, and

Amon—were *off-limits*. The Jews therefore had to go around these lands and approach the land ruled by Sichon, king of the Emorites.

The Jews asked Sichon if they could pass through his land. Not only did Sichon refuse their request, but he also led his nation into battle against the Jews. The Jews had no choice but to fight back. They won the battle and took possession of Sichon's land.

For some odd reason, the king of a second country, Bashan, thought he could defeat the Jews. He attacked, and just like Sichon before him, he lost the battle and his land. The lands of the Emorites and the Bashanites were given to the tribes of Reuben, Gad, and half the tribe of Manasseh.

Thus ends the stories we find in this week's reading. Now it is time for Moses to look towards the future.

He spends time in this part of his farewell address defining the borders of Canaan and explaining which tribes will be given which part of the land. He is careful to emphasize that which he had said to the tribes in the book of Numbers. Men from the tribes of Reuben, Gad, and half of Manasseh, whose land will be on the eastern side of the Jordan River, must cross the river along with the other tribes and take part in the battle to conquer Canaan. Only after the land is conquered and divided among all the other tribes (a process that takes fourteen years) may the men of Reuben, Gad, and half of Manasseh return to their homes on the eastern bank of the Jordan.

In one last act of looking ahead, Moses tells Joshua—who will lead the nation into Israel—not to be fearful of the battles which he will face, "for it is the LORD your God who will battle for you."

Life Lessons from *Devarim*

Perhaps more than any other book in the Torah, the opening chapter of Deuteronomy sets the tone for the entire book. We immediately see how Moses is so careful with his words as he reviews the adventures and experiences of the Jewish people over the past forty years. And, as you will come to understand as you dig deeper into Deuteronomy, the life lessons from this week's reading serve as a kind of starting point for many of the other life lessons to come.

DEVARIM (DEUTERONOMY 1:1—3:22)

Things Are Not Always What They Seem

This is the fourth in the Curious Student's Guide series, and the goal of each has been to look for important life lessons in the weekly Torah readings. In doing so, we've looked at the reading each week as a whole and avoided intensely studying specific verses to explain specific words or phrases. This is not to suggest that textual study is not important. It's just that sometimes you can get so caught up in deciphering words and phrases that you forget to take a look at the big picture.

That being said, we are now about to embark on an exception to our rule. We need to very carefully look at and break down the first verse of this week's reading if we are to discover an important life lesson.

As we noted above, the opening verse of our reading tells us exactly when and where Moses begins his farewell address. This fact seems trivial. Why does when and where matter? It really doesn't, and that's why we need to look deeper into the verse.

According to the greatest of the biblical commentators, Rabbi Shlomo ben Yitzhak (better known as Rashi), this entire first verse is written in code. Why would Moses, who has spoken openly and honestly to the people for forty years, now need to speak to them in code? Let's try to answer this question with a real-life example.

Imagine that, last week or last month, you made a terrible mistake and did something really bad. It doesn't matter exactly what you did. Whatever it was, it was just bad. Your parents scolded you and maybe even punished you. How can they be sure you learned your lesson and won't make the same mistake again?

They could scold you again or speak harshly to you. "Remember what you did last month?" they might ask. Only to follow with, "that was awful. Don't do it again!"

Do you think your parents would try this? Probably not. Speaking harshly will just make you feel bad all over again, and that's not what they want. They want to help you avoid mistakes in the future. Reminding you is their goal. Helping you is one of their goals, too. And they certainly want to do so in a positive way!

That's why it's more likely they will search for a gentle, indirect way of helping you learn your lesson should you make a mistake.

This is exactly what Moses wants to accomplish when beginning his speech. He hopes to help people avoid repeating their past mistakes. So, he hints at those mistakes rather than addressing them directly. He understands that speaking gently and in a reassuring manner will work much better than harsh, direct criticism. By using code to gently criticize the people, Moses successfully gets his message across to them. He does even more, though. He also teaches the people an important life lesson about always speaking kindly to others, especially when offering constructive criticism.

Now that we understand the reason for Moses's code, let's see if we can crack it.

These are the words that Moses addressed to all of Israel on the other side of the Jordan: through the wilderness, in the Arabah near Suph, between Paran and Tophel, Laban, Hazeroth, and Di-zahab.

Phrase from Verse 1	Rashi's Explanation (Paraphrased)
These are the words	Moses knows that he must criticize some past behaviors of the Jewish people, especially when what they did angered God. But he loves the people and wants to help them improve, so he mentions their past sins indirectly.
To all Israel	Moses made sure that everyone was present for his speech. This way, no one could say that, had I been there, I would have answered him back! Everyone was there, and no one had a response to Moses's polite and coded criticism.
The wilderness	They were not actually in the wilderness, but in the plains of Moab. So why mention "the wilderness"? Because they made God angry in the wilderness when they said: "If only we had died by the hand of the LORD in the land of Egypt" (Exodus 16:3)
in the Arabah (the plains)	Here he hints at the sin of idol worship they committed through Baal Peor at Shittim in the plains of Moab. (Numbers 25:1–18)

Devarim (Deuteronomy 1:1—3:22)

near Suph	The name of this place is very similar to the Hebrew word for the Sea of Reeds, and Moses here indirectly scolds them for their rebelliousness at the Sea of Reeds when they said, "Was it for want of graves in Egypt that you brought us to die in the wilderness? What have you done to us, taking us out of Egypt?" (Exodus 14:11)
between Paran and Tophel, Laban	Rashi notes that, having gone through the whole Bible, he found no places named Tophel or Laban! But these names are similar to the Hebrew words meaning "harsh statements" and "white." With this, Moses is hinting at the harsh things the Jewish people said about the manna, which was white. (Numbers 21:5)
	As for Paran, this is a hint about what they had done in the wilderness of Paran through the spies.
Hazeroth	This is a reference to the story of Miriam, when she was struck with tzara'at when she spoke to Aaron about Moses separating himself from his wife. (Numbers 12: 1–15) It is as if Moses asks a rhetorical question: "You should learn a lesson from what God did to Miriam at Hazeroth when she was not careful with her words, and yet, even after that, you spoke against God?"
and Di-zahab	This place name could be translated as "enough gold," which hints to the golden calf they made out of the large amounts of gold they had at that time.

The Most Obvious Life Lessons

While we have just begun to look for life lessons in Deuteronomy, let's skip ahead and imagine that we have already reached its conclusion. By the end of the book, we will see that Moses shares many stories in his farewell address about the triumphs and tragedies of the Jew's forty-year journey through the Sinai wilderness. If we've been paying close attention, we will have noticed that Moses ignores some pretty big events from the past forty years, most notably, the story of the golden calf.

Why do you think this is? Answering this question brings us to the most obvious and most central of all the life lessons we learn from Deuteronomy.

Moses spends much of his farewell speech telling stories of the past for a simple reason. He wants to help the Jewish people avoid repeating mistakes they have made once they enter Canaan. But Moses is wise enough to know that there are some mistakes the people will probably not repeat, like worshipping idols.

How can he be so sure that the people won't build another golden idol in the future? Part of the answer involves how embarrassed and sorry the people felt after they realized what they had done. They were ashamed. They were heartbroken. And if you have even felt ashamed or heartbroken about something you did, you understand why the people never wanted to feel that way again, which means no more idols, golden or otherwise.

There were other mistakes that Moses was less certain the people would not repeat, like those they made when sending out spies to Canaan. When you stop and think about it, the decision to send out spies was not such a bad idea. If successful, the spies could have gathered important information that would have made the conquest of the land easier. In fact, Moses himself actually agreed to the idea! But for reasons that are unclear to this very day, the spies decided to exaggerate their reports about what they saw and then make up horrible stories to convince the people that they should stay in the Sinai wilderness instead of invading Canaan.[1] The people's mistake was to believe the spies rather than have faith that God would be

---

1. There is a view put forward by some biblical commentators that the spies were convinced that life in the wilderness was far superior to the mundane existence that they would face upon conquering the land. How so? In the wilderness, the people ate manna from heaven, drank water from Miriam's miraculous well, and saw God's presence perpetually hovering above the Mishkan. The spies mistakenly thought that life in the wilderness was a better way to be close to God and to serve Him. God, in the book of Exodus, makes clear that He had a different preference. He desired to dwell among the people, which is why He commanded them to build a Mishkan, where His presence could be seen and felt. By descending from Heaven to dwell among His people, God highlights the importance of life in this world, His desire is that people should lead normal lives in which they strive to better themselves and not seek to hide in the spiritual realms.

Devarim (Deuteronomy 1:1—3:22)

with them, just like He was during the Exodus from Egypt and just as He has been during their forty years in the wilderness.

Now, the Jewish people are camped once again at the border of Canaan and are preparing to invade the land, and Moses understands that they would likely want to send out spies. By retelling the story of the first spy mission, Moses is reminding the people to carefully consider any report this second group of spies might bring back. He also makes clear to the people why they will certainly be victorious: "Do not fear them, for it is the LORD your God who will battle for you."[2]

Moses is not the only one who wants to help people avoid repeating past mistakes. Your parents and teachers want the same thing for you! And you want this for your friends and siblings, too. This life lesson goes to the heart of Deuteronomy, and we will see examples of it throughout the book.

> Moses's retelling of the spy story worked. The Jewish people did not make the same mistake when Joshua sent out spies before invading Canaan. How do your parents help you avoid repeating past mistakes? Do they use stories like Moses did? Do they use rewards and treats instead? Or maybe something else?

Sharing is Hard

Sharing is hard, whether you're an adult or a child. It is especially hard when you are asked to share something special. For the Jewish people, after forty years in the wilderness, nothing was more important to them than the land God had promised them. Each person wanted a fair share of the land. (After all, isn't sharing all about fairness?) The question was, what is fair when it comes to dividing up the land among the twelve tribes?[3]

---

2. Deuteronomy 3:22.

3. Even though the tribe of Levi got no portion of the land (its inheritance was the privilege of serving as priests in the Mishkan and again in the temple), the land was still divided into twelve portions. Jacob had given Joseph the inheritance rights of the first born, which meant that his descendants received a

This was the challenge facing Moses, and we can learn a lot about sharing by looking at how he handled this situation.

When commanding Moses to divide up the land among the people, God seems to emphasize fairness, but He is less than clear in what exactly this means:

> The LORD spoke to Moses, saying, "Among these shall the land be apportioned as shares, according to the listed names: with larger groups increase the share, with smaller groups reduce the share. Each is to be assigned its share according to its enrollment."[4]

If we stop and think carefully about these verses, we can see that there are two ways to divide the land in a fair manner. The first would be to give each of the twelve tribes an equal portion in the land. This is what a parent would typically do when leaving something to his or her children: give each child the same amount. There was one catch, which you will understand right away when looking at the chart below. Judah, the largest of the tribes, has many more members than Manasseh, the smallest of the tribes. Giving each tribe the same portion means that families in the larger tribes (like Judah) would receive less land than would families in the smaller tribes (like Manasseh).

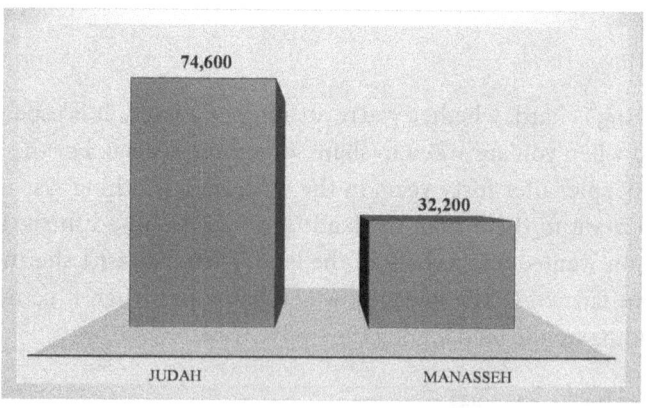

double portion in the land. This was done by giving his two grandsons Efraim and Menashe their own portion.

4. Numbers, 26:52–54.

Devarim (Deuteronomy 1:1—3:22)

The other way to divide the land fairly would be to give every family, no matter what tribe, the same amount of land. This would be very fair for individual families, but the larger tribes would of course end up with larger portions of the land. In the end, Moses concludes that it would be best to divide the land in a way that treated all families the same, and this is what the map Moses came up with looked like.

What lessons about sharing can we learn from all this?

First, when trying to share, we see that there can be more than one way to split things fairly. Different does not mean unfair.

Second, sometimes we need help determining the best and most fair way to share something. Imagine if the people themselves had tried to come up with a plan to divide the land. The leaders of the large tribes would have wanted the division to be done based on the size of the tribe. Families from the smaller tribes would have wanted the division to be done equally among the tribes, because that would have meant more land for their families.[5] Maybe the tribes would have worked things out; maybe not. Fortunately, Moses was there to take the lead. He did not favor one side over the other. He simply figured out what would be most fair and what would best satisfy God's command.

Third, sharing can involve compromise. Let's be honest. When it comes to sharing, we all want the biggest share. Sharing means everyone gets something, even if it's not exactly what we had hoped for. Perhaps not every tribe or every family agreed with Moses's plan, but they could see that it made sense, and they all worked together to follow the plan.

> *Whether it's with your siblings or your friends, you're probably asked to share a lot. Are you usually able to work things out with them, or do you need some help (like the Jewish people did when dividing up the land)? When you figure things out, are you generally satisfied, or are you a little sad or upset with the portion you get? What do you do to share these feelings?*

---

5. This is the very argument the thirteen original colonies had when trying to create a government for the newly independent United States. The larger colonies argued that they should have more representation because of their size. The smaller colonies wanted each of the thirteen to have the same number of representatives. In the end, they worked out a plan, called the Connecticut Compromise, which shared power fairly between the large and small states.

Va'etchanan

Deuteronomy 3:23—7:11

Summary of This Week's Reading

In this week's reading, we see, broadly speaking, Moses continuing to explain the importance of following God's commandments. Part of this involves sharing with the people the rewards for obeying God's words and the punishments for not listening to God.

The reading begins with Moses recounting how he begged God to allow him entry into Israel. (According to the Talmudic sages, Moses offered 515 different prayers as part of his effort to change God's mind about not letting him into the land of Israel!) God is firm in His decision. No land of Israel for Moses. But God does allow Moses to climb a mountain from where he can see the Promised Land.

It seems that Moses here is using himself as an example of the importance of following God's law and never adding to or taking away from it. (Remember, Moses was punished according to most opinions for hitting the rock instead of speaking to it.[1]) Moses uses another example, the Baal Peor incident,[2] to further remind the people of the good that comes to those who remain faithful to God.

---

1. Numbers 20.

2. As we read in Numbers 25:1–9, Baal Peor was an idol worshiped by the Moabites. On their way to the land of Canaan, when the Jews were near areas where this idol was worshipped, some Jewish men began to worship Baal Peor. The men who did so were judged by God, and many (24,000!) died in a plague as a result.

Moses next talks about the importance of the Torah. He discusses the wisdom it contains and the just laws it sets forth. He stresses that a commitment to the Torah will help the people remain close to God. To prove his point, Moses reminds the people of the day God gave them the Torah and describes for those who were not there (the children and grandchildren of those who left Egypt forty years earlier) how awesome that day truly was.

Having reminded the people of their encounter with God at Mount Sinai, Moses goes on to repeat and review the words God Himself spoke at that time. What is so very interesting about Moses's reteaching of these "Ten Utterances"[3] is the way he phrases them now. In certain key places, the version of the commandments written on those two tablets found in Moses's farewell address is different from the version of these utterances found in the book of Exodus.[4] (We will discuss in detail below some of the most important of these differences.) Moses concludes this portion of his farewell address by stressing the special connection the Jewish people have with God. One proof of this, says Moses, is the fact that the Jews are the only nation God personally delivered from slavery and the only people to whom God personally revealed Himself.

This week's reading includes an important commandment only now being given to the Jewish people because it will only go into effect when the Jews conquer the land of Canaan. This commandment establishes cities of refuge for those who inadvertently but carelessly cause the death of another person. Moses himself designates three of these cities on the eastern side of the Jordan River. Joshua will set up another three on the western side of the Jordan River once the conquest of Canaan is complete.

Our reading also contains one of Judaism's most important prayers: the first section of the Shema prayer. Part of what makes it so special is that it teaches the importance of belief (not just believing in God but loving Him as well) and of action (by teaching some

---

3. I discuss the nature of the words God uttered at Sinai in great detail in *A Curious Student's Guide to Exodus* in the chapter entitled "Commandments or Utterances: What's the Difference?"

4. Exodus 20.

Va'etchanan Deuteronomy 3:23—7:11

of Judaism's best known and most important commandments, namely the wrapping and wearing of tefillin, hanging the mezuzah, and Torah study).

Our reading concludes with Moses sharing God's promise to give the Jewish people a land filled with much goodness (often described as "flowing with milk and honey"). Moses urges them never to forget the Creator who provided them with this remarkable land and all its blessings. And to make clear that this land is God's special gift to the Jewish people, Moses tells them that they are to destroy the inhabitants of Canaan along with their idols.

Life Lessons from *Va'etchanan*

When people talk about Jewish beliefs and rituals, there are certain texts that are always part of the discussion. Two of them—the "Ten Utterances"[5] and the first paragraph of the Shema prayer—are found in this week's reading. There are many life lessons to be learned from each. Let's try and focus on a few of the more obvious ones.

Something New and A Little Crazy

The commandments that were inscribed on the two tablets God gave to Moses at Mount Sinai contained things that many people living at that time would have considered radical. Things like the belief in one God (an idea we will discuss in greater detail at the end of this chapter) and the Sabbath, for example, were both big departures from how things were at the time.

Let's talk about the Sabbath.

Idol worshippers throughout the ages built altars and temples to their gods. Some of these temples are still standing today, perhaps most famously the Parthenon in Athens, Greece.[6]

---

5. While often referred to as "the Ten Commandments," the proper translation of the Hebrew name for the words God spoke at Mount Sinai (*Aseret Hadibrot*) is "the Ten Utterances."

6. The Parthenon, a marble temple built between 447 and 432 BCE during the height of the ancient Greek Empire, was dedicated to the Greek goddess Athena.

Structures such as the Parthenon show that these ancient people understood they could dedicate special places to the worship of their gods. They considered such places to be holy. For them (and for the Jews themselves), God's command to build a *Mishkan* (the Tabernacle) where He could be worshipped and sacrifices could be offered to Him made perfect sense. In those days, serving your idol or worshipping the one true God took place in a special, holy place.

The Sabbath was something completely new and unheard of. It was to be a day on which the Jewish people set aside their day-to-day concerns and activities. They were to use this day for worshipping God and for reflecting on their relationship with God. In other words, the very notion of the Sabbath teaches us that holiness is not limited to a particular physical space. Time itself can be made holy.[7]

Jews who observe the Sabbath strive to make it a special and unique day. Work, of course, is forbidden on the Sabbath.[8] This

---

7. For parents wishing to explore this idea further, a wonderful resource is Abraham Joshua Heschel's *The Sabbath* (New York: Farrar, Straus, and Giroux, 2005 [orig. 1951]).

8. Jewish law forbids physical labor on the Sabbath. It also forbids what it considers to be "creative" activities, which includes things like building, drawing and painting, and even the use of electricity. To further safeguard the

makes it easier to set aside time for prayer and study, activities meant to enhance the holiness of the day. School work should be avoided because it is a weekday activity. (Some might argue that it should be avoided because it is a form of work for school-aged children.)

But in their desire to heighten the holiness of the Sabbath, Jews try to elevate even the most basic parts of their day to make these holy, too. How so? Jewish Sabbath observers wear special clothes in honor of the Sabbath. They prepare three elaborate meals (one for Friday night and two more for the next day) with special foods to honor the Sabbath. The conversations around their dinner tables are different. People try not to talk about work or school, because weekday activities (be it doing them or discussing them) are to be avoided on the Sabbath. Finally, Sabbath observers make it a point to walk leisurely to their synagogues. (Traditional Sabbath observance does not allow people to travel in cars.) Rushing here and there is what people do during the week, not on the Sabbath.

Of the many commandments God revealed at Mount Sinai, perhaps none has been more universally accepted than the Sabbath. The three worldwide religions that worship the one true God—Judaism, Christianity, and Islam—all observe a Sabbath day.[9] By doing so, these religions have embraced the idea that time can be as holy and special as any synagogue, church, or mosque. What was once considered a radical, if not impossible idea, became over the centuries a defining characteristic for these religions and their followers.

> *What things do you do (or avoiding doing) to make your Sabbath special? Are there other things you could do (or not do) to make your Sabbath even more special?*

---

holiness of the day, the Talmudic sages forbid financial activities and the use of money on the Sabbath.

9. The Jewish Sabbath is observed on Saturdays (or, to be more precise, from sunset on Friday until sunset on Saturday). Christians observe the Sabbath on Sundays, and Muslims, on Fridays.

Remembering and Observing

Commanding the Jewish people to make time holy on the Sabbath day, as God did at Mount Sinai, was not as simple as it might seem. How exactly does one do that? God gave the people some guidance with the words He chose to include in the Ten Utterances. But this, too, is a little complicated.

The Ten Utterances appear two times in the Torah. The first time is in the book of Exodus, where God says, "Remember (*zachor* in Hebrew) the sabbath day and keep it holy."[10] In his farewell address, Moses reviews the Ten Utterances with the people, but there he describes the commandment about the Sabbath in this way: "Observe (*shamor* in Hebrew) the sabbath day and keep it holy."[11]

At this point, you are probably asking, what is the difference between remembering and observing? More important, you should be asking, why did Moses change the language of God's commandment?

The Talmudic sages spent a good amount of time addressing this second question, and they concluded (based on a long-standing oral tradition) that the two verses—"Remember the sabbath day" and "Observe the sabbath day"—were spoken by God simultaneously (that is, at the same time). These sages were not bothered by the miraculous nature of this (after all, no human can speak two things at once, nor can any person hear and understand two things at once). From the fire and smoke to the lightning and thunder to God's voice itself, the entire Mount Sinai experience was miraculous! That's why, for the sages, there were more pressing questions, like what do we learn from "remember/*zachor*"? What do we learn from "observe/*shamor*"? How do the two differ?

Using the word "observe" when talking about the Sabbath is understandable. Observe covers all the most basic laws of the Sabbath, from the negative (which means not doing certain things, like working and cooking) to the positive (which means doing things, like praying and studying and having special meals). Practically speaking, God could not give the Jewish people any of the

10. Exodus 20:8.
11. Deuteronomy 5:12.

Sabbath commandments without the language of observe (or, as some translate *shamor*, keep).

Remembering is a little harder to understand. If a person is observing the Sabbath by not working and with prayer and study, what is there to remember? This individual is already involved with the Sabbath! One answer is that remembering has nothing to do with the day itself. It is all about remembering and looking forward to the Sabbath throughout the week. This explains why the Hebrew language does not have words like Sunday and Monday for the days of the week. Instead, Sunday is *Yom Rishon*, literally, the first day.[12] Monday is *Yom Sheni*, the second day. And what are we counting down to? The Sabbath, of course. Jews have other ways of looking forward to Shabbat. Grocery shopping is one example. Imagine a Jewish family food shopping on Wednesday (or the fourth day in Hebrew). They are in the bakery section of the store and see the most delicious looking cake. Buying that cake, but then saving it for the special Sabbath meal on Friday night, would be a way of remembering the Sabbath.

Here perhaps is the best way to think about it. You know how much you look forward to your birthday, sometimes even counting

---

12. In the Jewish calendar, the seventh day, Saturday, is the Sabbath, which makes Sunday the first day of the week.

the days until it arrives? That sense of excitement and anticipation is what it means to remember the Sabbath.

Now perhaps we can explain why Moses changes the language of the Ten Utterances in his farewell speech. God may have miraculously said "remember and observe" at the same time, but in the written text as it appears for the first time in Exodus, God emphasizes "remember." Learning to keep the Sabbath, as the Jews had to do in the desert, must have been hard. So many things they were used to doing daily (like starting fires) could not be done on the Sabbath. Big changes like this can be difficult. So, God, by using "remember," may well have been trying to build a sense of excitement around the Sabbath. And once they got the hang of it, keeping the Sabbath in the desert must have been pretty straightforward, as God's presence was always visible in the clouds of glory that hovered over the *Mishkan*. It is easy to follow the rules when you see that someone is watching you. Especially when that someone is God.

When Moses stands before the Jewish people as his days ended, he understands that life will be very different for the people once they enter Canaan. God's presence will not be so visible, which means the people will have to rely on their hearts and their faith, and not their eyes, when it comes to recognizing God. This is why Moses emphasizes "observe." It is as if he is saying to the people, "God's presence may no longer be hovering above the *Mishkan*, but He is still with us, still watching us. Just as you were careful to observe the Sabbath in the desert, be sure to be just as careful once you enter Canaan."

> *Do you act differently if you know your parents or teachers are watching you? If so, how so?*

The Reason Why Matters

Moses makes one other big change in language when discussing the Sabbath in his farewell address. In Exodus, God gives a very logical reason for the commandment of the Sabbath.

> Six days you shall labor and do all your work, but the seventh day is a sabbath of the LORD your God: you shall not do any work—you, your son or daughter, your male or female slave, or your cattle, or the stranger who is within your settlements. For in six days the LORD made heaven and earth and sea, and all that is in them, and He rested on the seventh day; therefore the LORD blessed the sabbath day and hallowed it.[13]

Here, God tells the Jewish people to rest on the seventh day, the Sabbath, because He, too, rested on the seventh day after spending six days creating the heavens and earth.[14] By keeping the Sabbath and resting on the seventh day, the Jewish people demonstrate their belief in God as the creator of the universe.

In this week's Torah reading, as Moses stands before the Jewish people, he thinks how different things will be once they enter Canaan. The daily miracles the people have grown used to will no longer be there: no manna from heaven to feed them; no well to provide them water; no clouds of glory over the *Mishkan* to remind them that God's presence is among them. Additionally, the war to conquer Canaan will not be easy.[15] Moses realizes that all these might be distractions for the people when it comes to keeping the Sabbath. Their new lives will be hard, and creation as a reason for keeping the Sabbath, logical as it may be, seems very distant. Moses senses that the people need a reason for keeping the Sabbath that they can relate to, and he knows exactly what it is.

> Six days you shall labor and do all your work, but the seventh day is a sabbath of the LORD your God; you shall

---

13. Exodus 20:9–11.

14. Most Jewish biblical commentators do not believe the universe was literally created in six twenty-four-hour periods. Instead, they understand the word "day" as a metaphor for a much longer period of time (just how long is less clear). That said, the age of the universe is much discussed among religious writers and scholars, Jewish and non-Jewish alike. One of my favorite books on the topic is Gerald L. Schroeder's *The Science of God: The Convergence of Scientific and Biblical Wisdom* (New York: Free Press, 2009 [orig. 1997]).

15. As the book of Joshua tells us, it takes the people seven years to conquer the land and another seven years to divide it among the twelve tribes.

not do any work—you, your son or your daughter, your male or female slave, your ox or your ass, or any of your cattle, or the stranger in your settlements, so that your male and female slave may rest as you do. Remember that you were a slave in the land of Egypt and the LORD your God freed you from there with a mighty hand and an outstretched arm; therefore the LORD your God has commanded you to observe the sabbath day.[16]

If keeping the Sabbath involves acknowledging the greatness of God, Moses gives the people what is for them a real example of God's greatness as well as His mastery over the world. Many of the Jews about to enter Canaan saw the miracles that allowed them to leave Egypt (the ten plagues and the splitting of the sea) with their own eyes. Those who did not heard stories about these miracles from their parents and grandparents. For this generation, the Exodus was a more real demonstration of God's power—and thus a better rationale for the Sabbath—than the creation of the universe.

What lesson can we learn from Moses's change in language?

Sometimes when we are asked to do things, the reason why may not be important. But with challenging things or things that we are asked to do over and over, understanding why can make it easier. This may not be true for every person and for every task but knowing why certainly seemed to work for the generation about to enter the land of Canaan. It helped them continue observing the Sabbath and continue making it a priority in their lives.

One God, Our God

Schools, sports teams, even countries often have mottos or sayings that describe what they're all about or what they stand for. For instance, the traditional motto of the United States, which is part of the country's national emblem, is *E pluribus unum*, a Latin phrase which means "out of many, one."

---

16. Deuteronomy 5:13–15.

Va'etchanan Deuteronomy 3:23—7:11

The Shema prayer is, in a sense, the motto of the Jewish people. Look carefully at its opening words: "Hear, O Israel! The Lord who is our God, He, the Lord, is one." This statement is an important part of the morning and evening prayers said by Jews all over the world. It is also the last thing Jews are to say right before they go to sleep at night. (In many homes, parents recite it nightly with their children as part of their bedtime ritual.) What makes the Shema prayer a Jewish motto are two very important ideas it contains.

First, by reciting Shema, a Jew declares that his or her God is unique, that He is the one and only true God. The belief in one God is what Judaism is all about. While most of us see the idea of believing in one God as common (after all, Christians and Muslims believe in one God, just like Jews do), this was not always the case. When Moses included the Shema in his farewell address, he was reminding the Jewish people that they lived in a world where the other nations worshipped idols and false gods. Declaring the belief in one God was unique and, some might say, radical.

Second, by reciting Shema, a Jew makes clear that he or she believes only in the God who created the world and who rules over it. For some, this belief is closely tied to their observance of the commandments. They see observing the Sabbath or the Jewish dietary laws as an expression of their belief in God. Others express their belief in God by the good deeds they do and by their commitment to making the world a better place.

Both groups can and do proclaim their belief in God with the same Shema prayer. This makes sense because Shema begins with "Hear, O Israel." The word "Israel" refers to the Jewish people as well as to the individuals who make up that people. And this call to all of Israel, both the nation and the people, makes Shema the perfect motto for Judaism.

> *In addition to its motto, the United States also has a symbol—the bald eagle—that represents the country's beliefs. If you were to create a "national emblem" for Judaism, what image would you choose to go along with the Shema "motto"? Why this image?*

Eikev

Deuteronomy 7:12—11:25

Summary of This Week's Reading

In a certain sense, Moses's farewell address is a kind of "pep talk" to the Jews in which he reminds them again and again that they need not fear the Canaanite armies they will encounter because God will help them in their conquest of the land. This week's reading is a continuation of the pep talk Moses began in our previous readings, so it makes sense that it begins with a promise: if the Jews observe God's commandments, then they will be blessed in many ways, including the utter defeat of their Canaanite enemies. Moses goes on to instruct the people that, after their victory, they must destroy all the idols they find in Canaan.

Moses then discusses their forty-year journey through the desert, highlighting the many tests and miracles they experienced. Moses also describes many of the wonderful features of the land of Israel, and he informs them that they must bless God after they eat and are satisfied. (This, of course, is the source for Birkat Hamazon, the special grace after meals traditionally recited by Jews.)

Being the good leader that he is, Moses worries that the victories and many blessings he just promised the people might cause them to forget and recognize the One (that is, God) who will make all these happen. Moses therefore warns the people that doing so would be a terrible mistake and would have terrible consequences. To prove his point, Moses makes it clear that the Jews will not inherit the land of Israel simply because they are (or hope to be) a good and righteous people. Rather, their future success is linked to the promise God made to the Patriarchs, namely that their descendants will become a great nation and will inherit the land of Israel. In fact, Moses reminds the people of the many times they angered God while in the desert, placing special emphasis on the sin of the Golden calf, which was when God would have annihilated the Jews had Moses not begged God to spare them.

Having mentioned the Golden calf, Moses recalls how at that time he smashed the two tablets he had received at Mount Sinai and how God commanded him to carve two new tablets upon which the words of the Ten Utterances were engraved. Another important detail of that story, one which Moses repeats here, is that God chose the tribe of Levi to serve as priests in the Mishkan. Becoming priests was a special reward to the Levites who, because of their devotion to God throughout the Golden calf incident, did not participate in the sin.

The reminder of this week's reading has several important, but not necessarily related items. For example, Moses tells the people that they must love and fear God and serve Him. The reason, while obvious to all, was worth repeating. Their love and service are reflections of God having chosen the Jews to be His treasured nation. Moses also reminds the people that the land of Israel always depends on God for the rains their crops need, which explains why, says Moses, the land is always under God's watchful eyes.

This final portion of the reading contains several important commandments related to certain rituals that Jews observe to this day, such as the second paragraph of the Shema prayer, tefillin, mezuzah, and teaching Torah to children.

Life Lessons from *Eikev*

This week we will focus on two very important life lessons. Some might think the first one is new, but it's not. Others might think the second one is so obvious that it's not worth talking about. Nothing could be farther from the truth.

Pay It Forward

Have you ever heard people talk about "paying it forward"? The phrase "pay it forward" comes from the title of a book written by Catherine Ryan Hyde in 1999. The main character in that book was a seventh-grade student named Trevor. One day at school, Trevor was given an assignment by his social studies teacher. Each student in the class was to come up with a plan that could help make the world a better place. To successfully complete the assignment, students had to follow the plans they created.

Trevor comes up with something he calls "pay it forward." It is a simple—but brilliant—plan, and here is how it works. When a friend did a favor for Trevor, he did not repay the favor to his friend. Instead, he took it upon himself to do a favor for three other people. The idea was that each of these individuals would do three favors for three other people, who in turn would do favors for three more people, and so on and so on.

What started as a plot point in a work of fiction grew to become a thing in real life. You can find stories in the news and online almost daily about someone "paying it forward." There is even a Pay It Forward Day, which is a worldwide celebration of kindness that takes place every year on April 28.[1]

Paying it forward is not as hard as it might seem. Some examples include simple acts like holding the door/elevator for others, doing the dishes, making your bed, treating someone else while you treat yourself to ice cream or a cookie, and picking up trash along your street or in the park. It could even be as easy as smiling at someone and giving them a compliment.

By now you might be thinking, what a great idea, but what does this have to do with this week's Torah reading? A lot actually.

Catherine Ryan Hyde may have come up with the phrase "pay it forward," but the idea behind paying it forward has been a Jewish tradition for generations. We refer it as *"zechut avot"* (the merits of our ancestors), and this term describes the positive influence the good deeds of one's ancestors can have on an individual.

This is what Moses had in mind when he tells the people they will not inherit the land of Israel simply because they are (or hope to be) a good and righteous people. To be clear, it is always important to do your best to be a good person, and the Jewish people who were about to enter Canaan certainly understood this. What Moses was trying to explain was that others "paid it forward" for the Jews. Their ancestors, the Patriarchs and Matriarchs, did many, many great things in their service of God. God recognized this by promising to the Patriarchs that their descendants would become a great nation and would inherit the land of Israel.

Did the Jews of Moses's time do their part? Did they serve God faithfully and fight hard to conquer Canaan? Absolutely, but without the Patriarchs and Matriarchs paying it forward, their efforts might have fallen short.

> What are two or three things you can do this week to pay it forward? How can you encourage your friends and family to also do something this week to pay it forward?

---

1. Pay It Forward Day was founded in 2007 by Australian Blake Beattie. It has grown exponentially since then. As of 2021, more than eighty countries participate in Pay It Forward Day. In the US, there are over 100 related state and city proclamations. See https://payitforwardday.com/ for more details.

Consequences to Your Actions

Before we consider the second life lesson from this week's reading, we're going to pause for a moment and learn a new word: corollary. Corollary is a word used to describe a result that is the natural consequence of something else. For example, your increased love of doughnuts is a corollary to the recent opening of a new doughnut shop in your neighborhood.

Let's put our new word to use in thinking about Moses's farewell address.

Moses spends a good bit of time this week talking about the consequences of the people's actions. When retelling the story of the Golden calf, he reminds the people of the positive consequence that occurred to the tribe of Levi—receiving the honor of serving as priests in the *Mishkan*—because they took no part in creating or worshipping the Golden calf. Positive consequences to our actions can be a "corollary" to paying it forward. Paying it forward involves doing something good, and the hope and expectation is that it will lead to additional acts of goodness.

The reverse holds true, too, as Moses makes clear to the people. He tells them (in the strongest of terms) that not obeying God's commandments will have terrible consequences: the worst being exile from their homeland. Sadly, the Jews did not heed Moses's words. Hundreds of years later, the people regularly committed the most serious of sins, including idol worship and murder. God sent prophets to remind the people of Moses's words and to warn them of the consequences that would result from their sinful behavior. They ignored these warnings, and, in the year 586 BCE, the armies of Babylonia invade Israel, destroy the temple, and send the Jewish people into exile far from their homes for seventy years.

Fast forward several hundred years. The Jews have returned from their exile in Babylonia and have rebuilt the temple. But they again forget Moses's warning from this week's reading. They again engage in sinful acts. This time it is hating each other without cause. The temple is destroyed once again (this time in the year 70 CE), and the Jews are sent back into exile.[2]

That there are consequences to our actions seems like an obvious concept. You just need to look around the world you live in or maybe reflect on things that have happened in your own life for this to become clear. But in his farewell address, Moses takes nothing for granted. This would be his final message to the Jewish people. He wants only good for them, and if saying the obvious would help them do good, then that is what Moses is going to do. Indeed, he did just that.

Learning and remembering this simple fact—that there are always consequences to our actions—just might be one of the most important life lessons in the entire book of Deuteronomy.

---

2. The Talmudic sages knew their history well, and they knew the stories of the destruction of both temples. When comparing the two, they reached an amazing and surprising conclusion (words in italics are the literal translation of the talmudic text): "Considering that the people during *the Second Temple* period *were engaged in Torah* study, observance of *mitzvot, and acts of kindness,* and that they did not perform the sinful acts that were performed in the First Temple, *why was* the Second Temple *destroyed?* It was destroyed *due to* the fact *that there was wanton hatred* during that period. This comes *to teach you that* the sin of *wanton hatred is equivalent to the three* severe *transgressions: Idol worship, forbidden sexual relations, and bloodshed."*

Re'eh

Deuteronomy 11:26—16:17

Summary of This Week's Reading

This week's reading begins with Moses telling the Jewish people that they can receive either blessings or curses: blessings if they obey God's commandments, and curses if they don't. To show how seriously the people should take these blessings and curses, Moses tells them that they are to conduct a special ceremony in which they repeat these blessings and curses to each other once they enter the land of Canaan.[1] And, as a further safeguard against any potential curses, Moses reminds the people that they must destroy all idols they find when they enter the Holy Land.

Moses also discusses other things that must be done when the people enter Canaan. For example, he tells them that God will pick a specific place (which Moses does not name, but we all know is Jerusalem) where His Presence will rest (like in the Mishkan in the desert). All sacrifices must be offered in this holy city, and the meat from the sacrifices must be eaten there as well. However, God does permit the people to slaughter cattle and eat meat in their homes so long as they never eat the blood of the animal.

Moses often speaks of the dangers of Canaan. He has already advised the people against idol worship. Now he gives the people additional warnings, such as those about false prophets. Any person who claims to be a prophet with a message from God to worship

---

1. The details of this ceremony are set forth in Deuteronomy 27:11–16.

idols must be put to death. This is true even if the person performs supernatural acts or accurately predicts the future. Moses goes on to tell the people that anyone who tries to get others to worship idols is also to be put to death whether or not they claim to be a prophet.

Moses moves on from idol worship to remind the people that they are God's children. As such, we must take special care of our bodies and avoid decorating our bodies with things like tattoos or other forms of mutilation.

Next comes a list of kosher animals and non-kosher birds. Moses is careful to teach the people how to tell the difference between kosher and non-kosher animals and fish. He finishes his discussion of the dietary laws by reviewing the prohibitions against eating meat from an animal which was not properly slaughtered and against cooking meat with milk.

Moses concludes this portion of his farewell address with two important commandments that apply only to life in the land of Israel.

First, the Jewish people are to observe every seventh year as a Shemitah (Sabbatical) Year. Not only are the people forbidden from farming (in order to let the land rest), but all outstanding loans are to be forgiven. Moses senses that people will not want to lend money to the poor among them if the Shemitah year is approaching. He tells them that they must always help the poor and do so with a happy heart, before, during, and after the Shemitah year.

The second commandment involves the male firstborn of kosher cattle. These animals belong to God and are to be offered as sacrifices in the Temple. Part of the animal is burnt on the altar, and the priests are given the remainder to eat.

Our reading concludes with a discussion of the festivals of Passover, Shavuot (Pentecost in English), and Sukkot (or Tabernacles). Moses reviews some laws regarding each of these holidays. He emphasizes that the people are to rejoice and be happy on all of them and that all males who can make the journey must come to Jerusalem to celebrate each holiday.

Life Lessons from *Re'eh*

This week's reading gives us some special insights about the belief in God as well as practical details about Jewish dietary laws. Both are core principles of Judaism, which is why we will consider each of them carefully.

Seeing versus Hearing

Over the years, educators have developed different models to help define and explain the many ways in which we learn. One of the most popular models, called Visual Auditory and Kinesthetic (VAK), was developed by Walter Burke Barbe in 1979.[2] This model can be explained quite simply. Visual learners learn and remember new information by seeing it. Auditory learners do this by hearing it. And Kinesthetic learners need to move to retain new information.

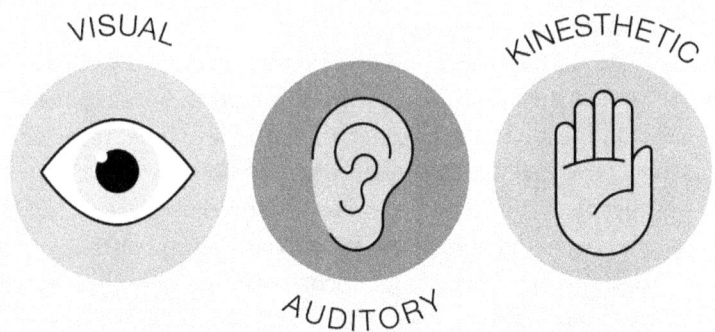

The point of Barbe's research and observations is quite simple. It does not matter how students learn, be it math, science, history, or literature. What matters most is that teachers recognize these learning differences and help students learn in a way that works best for them.

---

2. In 1987, Neil Fleming expanded on this model to include Reading and Writing (thus turning VAK into VARK—Visual, Auditory, Reading & Writing, and Kinesthetic).

Perhaps this is how your classes at school are organized. The idea is that students should be allowed and encouraged to find a learning style that best suits them. Seeing it versus hearing it makes no difference so long as the student is successful in mastering the lesson and the material it contains.

While this approach works very well in school, it creates certain problems when the topic is God and learning to believe in Him.

In his farewell address, Moses is aware of the differences between seeing and hearing when it comes to God. He even begins this week's reading with the word "see"! Moses knows that there are some among the Jewish people standing before him who saw for themselves the miracles that happened in Egypt when God sent the ten plagues and split the Sea of Reeds.[3] Many more people saw firsthand the miracles that occurred daily during their forty-year journey through the desert: the manna that fell from heaven each day to feed them; the water that always flowed from the rock that followed them in the desert; and the clouds of glory that hovered above the *Mishkan* indicating God's presence among the Jewish people.

When a person sees and experiences such open miracles, it is hard not to believe in God. And while God wants us to believe in Him, and while He truly hopes we will believe in Him, He does not force us to believe. God's plan when He created the world was to give people a choice: to believe or not to believe. There may be consequences to our choice, but the choice is always ours.

Moses understands this, which is why he describes things from the previous forty years using language like "as your eyes saw." Those who left Egypt saw the sea split. They saw God's presence at Mount Sinai. They do not need to hear about these things to remember them or learn important lessons from them. Their seeing makes it easy to believe in God.

But what about the future generations, the children and grandchildren of those who left Egypt and beyond? The Exodus is

---

3. Most English translations of the Bible's Exodus story mistranslate the Hebrew phrase *yam suf* as the Red Sea. The correct translation for the body of water God split for the Jews upon their exodus from Egypt is the Sea of Reeds.

at the core of their history. The Mount Sinai experience is central to their religious beliefs. Since they didn't see it for themselves, all these people have is hearing, and their choice to believe in God or not is, in a sense, based solely upon hearing.

Maybe you're wondering whether the people who saw all these miracles believed more deeply in God than those who only heard about the miracles. That's a very good question. And a very important one. Let's try to answer it as simply as possible.

Belief is not based on seeing miracles. Seeing something makes it real. People who believe in God choose to believe in Him without ever seeing Him or hearing Him. How do such people know God is real? Because their belief is strong enough for them to feel God without seeing Him or seeing the kinds of miracles He did for the Jews when they left Egypt. That's why, if today there were open miracles like in the old days, the choice of whether or not to believe in God would disappear. Seeing changes everything. Once you see something, it becomes a matter of fact, not belief.

All this makes believing in God very special. It can make it difficult, too.

Speaking for myself, I know there are things in life that I cannot see, like gravity or the air I breathe. But there are scientific proofs for both, so I know for a fact that they are real. I cannot see God. No one has shown me a proof that God exists. As often as I speak to Him, He has yet to speak back to me.[4] Despite all this, I know God exists and that He is real. My belief in Him is that strong. And were I to witness an open miracle like those in the Bible, my belief would not change. It would not be any stronger because of such miracles.

---

4. Speaking to God, be it in the form of a prayer or a simple conversation, is often misunderstood by many people. They think that just because God does not answer prayers, He does not hear them. Judaism teaches that God always hears our prayers. When or how He chooses to answer those prayers is a different matter. Sometimes there is no answer. Sometimes the answer may be obvious (like when a sick friend or family member gets well). And at other times, the answers are there. We just need to be listening well enough to hear and understand the answer, especially because such answers are never given to us in words.

Know that I am not alone with my faith. There are literally millions and millions of people around the world who believe like I do. (Maybe you're one of them!) We are the people Moses had in mind when he shifts from talking about seeing to talking about hearing in his farewell address. Hearing means more than listening. It means being open-minded and willing to hear new ideas. It means paying attention to the world around us.

The truth is, there are miracles happening around you every day, even those with scientific explanations, like the flowers blooming each spring year after year and like the babies who are born daily and grow up to live happy and productive lives. If you take it all in, hearing and seeing it, it is possible to recognize God's presence in so many aspects of your life.

In the end, how you learn that two plus two equals four makes no difference. You can see it by counting on your fingers. You can listen to your teacher explain it. You can even count the beats in a song to help you figure it out. But we can't see God or touch Him or listen to the rhythms of His existence. What we have instead are God's commands and Moses's farewell address to teach and guide us as we listen to the words and seek to hear God in them.

> *How would you define a miracle? Have you experienced miracles in your life?*

Nothing to Do with Health

Keeping kosher has long been one of the things that defines Judaism, and it is certainly one of the most important rituals Jews observe to this day. Nonetheless, of the Torah's many commandments, few are as misunderstood as the Jewish dietary laws.

Why is this?

Many people mistakenly believe that the Jewish dietary laws are all about "eating healthy." They point out that in ancient times, eating pork could easily lead to trichinosis, a stomach ailment whose symptoms usually include diarrhea (loose stool/poop), nausea (feeling of sickness in the stomach), fatigue, and stomach pain. This is why, these folks claim, God forbade the Jews from eating pork.

It's an interesting theory, but if trichinosis was the reason God banned pork, now that it is very uncommon for a person to get it from eating pork, shouldn't Jews be allowed to eat ham sandwiches and bacon? More fundamentally, if the dietary laws were concerned with health issues, why didn't God give the Jews other health-related commandments, like getting eight hours of sleep every night or exercising regularly or avoiding excessive eating and drinking or not smoking cigarettes? You get the point.

In reality, there is a simple explanation generally given for the dietary laws, and we can learn a lot from it, as it sheds light on how we ought to see our relationship with God.

Jews think of God as their Father in heaven. As such, they try to serve Him out of a sense of love. Like good children, they should always ask themselves, will my Father in heaven be happy with my actions? Will He be pleased? Will He be proud of me? But Jews also accept God as their king, a theme that is present in their New Year's prayers and rituals, when they refer to God as *Aveinu Malkeinu* (our Father, our King). Kings (and queens) often issue orders that they expect their servants to follow without question. God does, too, and there are some well-known commandments in the Torah that are never explained, such as the prohibition against wearing clothing made out of wool and linen (*shatnez*). No one is quite sure why God forbade the Jews from wearing such garments, but Jews don't wear them simply because God said so.

The Jewish dietary laws fall into this category. There is no reason given in the Torah why Jews can only eat animals that chew their cud[5] and have split hooves. Similarly, we don't know why Jews can only eat fish with fins and scales. This is the King's command, and the Jews, like loyal subjects, follow without question.

> *Serving God as a parent and a king involves a combination of love and awe (some might say fear). Listening to your parents combines both love and awe, too. Can you list some things you do for your parents just out of love? Some things you do out of respect? From both?*

Whose Stuff is it Anyways?

How much stuff do you have in your bedroom? A bed and some furniture for sure, but what about games and toys? Stuffed animals? Books? And what about your closet? It's surely full of clothes and shoes and who knows what else. It's all your stuff, or is it?

Think about that for a minute. The toys and clothes are yours, but your parents bought them for you, right? Like you, they think of all this stuff as yours, but if they wanted to, they could take some (or all) of these things from you, couldn't they? Maybe they even do so occasionally if you misbehave. So, if that's the case, whose stuff is it anyway?

These are interesting questions to be sure, and in a way, God asks the same questions of us.

When God finished creating our world, He gave control of it to humankind, as the verse says, "Be fertile and increase, fill the earth and master it."[6] He even gave the land of Israel to the Jewish people as a special gift. This means that everything in this world belongs to God, just like everything in your room can be said to

---

5. When animals such as cows or sheep chew the cud, they slowly chew their partly-digested food over and over again in their mouth before finally swallowing it.

6. Genesis 1:28.

belong to your parents. It's easy for people to forget this, just like it may be easy for you to sometimes forget how much stuff your parents have given you over the years. This is why God gives the Jewish people a special commandment called *Shemitah*.

Moses reviews the details of the Sabbatical year during his farewell address. He reminds the people that *Shemitah* is to be observed every seven years and that during the seventh year, all farming activities are forbidden, including plowing, planting, pruning, and harvesting. Certain things can be done, like watering, fertilizing, weeding, spraying, trimming, and mowing, but only to protect trees and other plants, not to improve their growth. Moses makes one additional and important point. Any fruits or herbs which grow on their own are considered ownerless and may be picked by anyone.

The Sabbatical year is not intended to improve the land, even though it is a known fact that allowing farmland to rest occasionally results in better crops. The purpose of *Shemitah* is to remind the Jews that the land is merely theirs to use, but not to truly own. The land really belongs to God, and *Shemitah* helps the Jewish people appreciate all that God has given them.

Sometimes, people only appreciate the things they have when those things are taken away from them. God, in his great wisdom, takes the land back every seven years so that the Jews can fully understand how special the land is and what a gift it really is!

> *Do you ever stop and thank your parents for everything they do and give you? If so, how do you show your appreciation? How often do you show your appreciation?*
> *Do you think you'd be more appreciative if your parents took away some of your stuff on a regular basis?*

Shoftim

Deuteronomy 16:18—21:9

Summary of This Week's Reading

The name of this week's reading, Shoftim (Judges in English), reflects the first commandment discussed in it, that is, the obligation to appoint judges in every city of Israel. Moses tells the people (and the future judges among them) that judges must always be fair in their decisions. While on the topic of judges, Moses adds that the people must follow the rulings of the Sanhedrin (the rabbinic supreme court) and the Oral Law. In fact, says Moses, a person who refuses to accept the Sanhedrin's authority can be sentenced to death by the court.

Moses next tells the people to crown a king after they enter Canaan.[1] Moses goes on to warn the future king not to have too many horses or wives and not to acquire too much personal wealth. The king must also write two Torah scrolls. One is kept in the palace and the other is to always remain with the king. It is meant to be a constant reminder to him to remain humble and to follow God's law.

There is a third type of leader, priests (kohanim in Hebrew), that Moses discusses. These priests, who must be descendants of Aaron (whom God personally selected to be the first priest), are not to receive a portion in the land of Israel, because, as Moses explains, "God is their inheritance." Instead, the priests are supported directly

---

1. As we will discuss below, it is unclear from the text if Moses is telling the people that they must appoint a king or that they may, if they wish, appoint a king.

(through contributions of crops and wool and from select portions of meat from animals slaughtered for private use) or indirectly (priests are entitled to the meat and hides of certain animals sacrificed in the Temple) by all the Jewish people.

Some activities, like witchcraft and fortune-telling, go against everything the priests stand for: that is, putting one's faith and trust in God. Moses therefore tells the people that such activities are forbidden, and he emphasizes that these activities are unnecessary. Why? Because the Jewish people are blessed with prophets who share God's messages to His people. This of course means that the people are to obey the words of the prophets.[2]

Moses then changes the subject and returns to the command to build cities of refuge for people who accidently or unintentionally cause the death of others. Moses commands the Jews to set up six such cities. He adds that when God expands the borders of the land (with the coming of the Messiah), they are to add another three cities of refuge.

Having discussed accidental deaths, Moses turns to the topic of intentional killings (murder). Moses teaches that a minimum of two witnesses are required to convict a person in a case involving murder. He adds that individuals who testify falsely in such cases receive the very punishment they sought for their innocent victim. (The end of our reading talks about what is to be done in the case of an unsolved murder.)

Moses concludes with one last topic: the rules of war. When a Jewish army goes out to war and approaches the battlefield, a priest selected specifically for this duty speaks to the soldiers. He must tell them not to fear the enemy, for God will be with them. He also explains who is not required to go out to battle. This list includes men who were recently engaged or married, men who had just built a new home, or men who were simply too afraid to go out to battle.

---

2. Sadly, the Jewish people did not always heed the words of the prophets, as we read in books like Jeremiah and Ezekiel. These prophets were sent by God to warn the people of the consequences of disobeying His commandments. In the end, the people ignored these warnings, and, as a result, the Temple was destroyed in 586 BCE and the people were exiled to Babylonia.

Moses adds a final note about war, and it is a very important commandment. Before a Jewish army can begin a war, they must first try to make peace with their enemies.³ Only if the enemy does not accept an offer of peace may the Jewish army attack. And while waging war and laying siege on a city, a Jewish army may not cut down fruit-bearing trees.

Life Lessons from *Shoftim*

In this week's reading, there are many commandments that will be important for the Jewish people once they conquer the land of Canaan, including laws about appointing judges, the obligation to follow rabbinic law and the words of the prophets, the obligations of a king, the laws of war, and the how to deal with unsolved murders. But the main theme of our reading is leadership, and in it, Moses describes different kinds of leaders: judges, kings, priests, and prophets. Moses uses these individuals to teach us about different character traits that help make good leaders (and good people, too). Let's see what some of them have to offer us.

Judges

Even if you've never been in a court (and chances are good that you never have been), you probably understand what judges do, because, when all is said and done, judges do one thing: they make decisions. If a crime has been committed, the job of a judge can be to look over the facts and decide if a person is innocent or guilty. If it's a case involving money, the judge looks over the facts and decides who owes whom what and how much.

It sounds simple enough, but the truth is, judges spend years studying the law, and the best judges also have years of experience to help them make good and correct decisions. Moses certainly recognizes this, but when he discusses in this week's reading the

---

3. If an enemy attacks first, there is obviously no obligation for the Jewish army to pursue peace negotiations. They always have the right to defend themselves against attacks.

importance of having judges and what's expected of them, he doesn't talk about training or experience. Moses instead focuses on what we would call character traits, or said differently, what type of person the judge must be. Here is how Moses explains it. He says:

> You shall not judge unfairly: you shall show no partiality; you shall not take bribes, for bribes blind the eyes of the discerning and upset the plea of the just.[4]

Showing no partiality means not taking sides. A judge must look upon all who stand before him or her as equals. The judge must listen carefully to both sides and consider what both have to say.

Not taking bribes means being honest. It also means understanding how important the role of a judge is in society and how a judge must always act in a way that make people trust him or her.

Maybe you think growing up to be a judge would be awesome, or maybe you have never even given it a single thought. It doesn't matter. What Moses expects of judges—to be fair and honest and always try to make good decisions—are things your parents and

---

4. Deuteronomy 16:19.

teachers probably expect of you. And they are certainly things we should all expect of ourselves.

> Have you ever had friends who were in an argument ask you to decide who's right? What did you do? Were you able to reach a decision? Do you think it was a fair and correct one?

Kings and Queens

Kings and queens seem to be everywhere in children's books and movies. Not so much in real life, but that hasn't always been the case. In ancient times, when Moses was giving his farewell address, most countries in the world were ruled by kings (and sometimes by queens). This was true even in more modern times, like in 1776 when the original thirteen colonies declared their independence from England, which was ruled by a king.

Being a king or queen in the ancient world (and even in more modern times) meant that your word was law. You decided what your subjects could or could not do. You decided what was right and what was wrong. And of course, because you made the law, the law did not apply to you. You, as king or queen, could do whatever you liked, whenever you liked.

When you read the Torah's commandments involving a Jewish king, it is not at all clear if God tells the Jews they must have a king to rule over them or if He says they may have a king. You understand the difference. If they *must* have a king, the Jewish people have no choice in how their country will be governed. If they *may* have a king, the people can decide if having a king is good or right for them.

But there is one thing God makes perfectly clear. A Jewish king (or queen) is not above the law. He or she must obey God's commandments, just like other people must. To show just how true this is, Moses tells the people that the king must always have a Torah scroll with him and that he should study it all the days of his life.[5] Why this need for a Torah scroll? Moses states it very plainly: "So that he may learn to revere the LORD his God, to observe faithfully every word of this Teaching as well as these laws."[6]

There's more.

As you can image, a king or queen whose word is law and who can do whatever they please is probably not a very humble person. They probably also don't understand limits, so they are often tempted to build huge palaces and amass great amounts of gold, silver, and precious jewels. (History shows that this is exactly what kings did!) Makes sense. If you think you can have anything in life, you're probably going to try to get everything in life.

Here, however, a Jewish king or queen is to act differently. Moses warns future Jewish kings about keeping their priorities straight. They are not, says Moses, to build excessive wealth, and he gives a very specific example of what he means: "he [the king] shall not keep many horses or send people back to Egypt to add to his horses."[7] Moses continues to warn these future kings about being obsessed with their own needs and pleasures, and he again gives a very specific example: a king is not to have too many wives![8]

5. Deuteronomy 17:18–19.
6. Deuteronomy 17:19.
7. Deuteronomy 17:16.
8. Two factors help us understand this warning. First, in ancient times, kings often had multiple wives. We see an excellent example of this in the Purim story, where King Ahasuerus had dozens of wives. Second, Jewish law at that time allowed men, be they kings or subjects, to have more than one wife. (About one thousand years ago, Jewish men opted to ignore this law and

Taken together, these warnings have a single goal: to make sure a Jewish king remains humble.[9]

None of us today are kings or queens, and few of us need be concerned about having too much gold or too many horses. But Moses's message to the future kings of Israel—be humble and keep your priorities straight—is one we should all take to heart.

> *Being humble can mean not being braggy about things you're good at. What things are you really good at? How do you stay humble when you talk about these things?*

---

marry only one wife.) Given all this, it makes great sense for Moses to tell Jewish kings not to take too many wives.

9. As the verse (17:20) makes clear, "Thus he will not act haughtily toward his fellows or deviate from the Instruction to the right or to the left, to the end that he and his descendants may reign long in the midst of Israel."

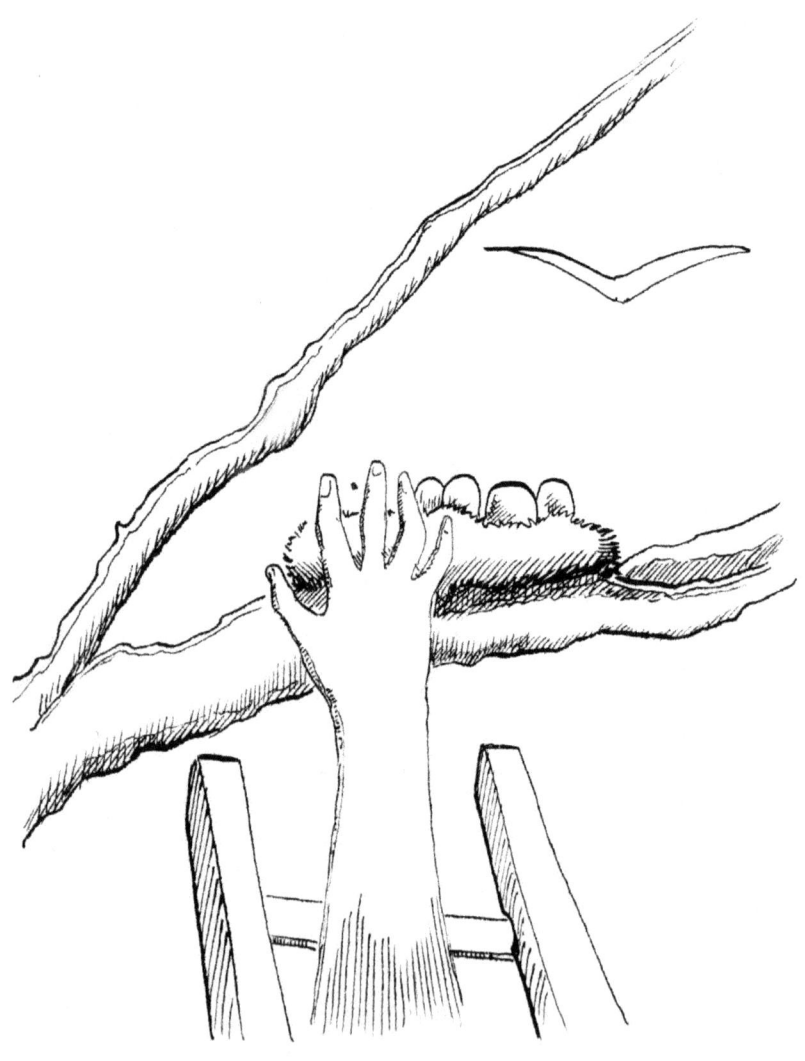

Ki Teitzei

Deuteronomy 21:10—25:19

Summary of This Week's Reading

This week's reading is difficult to summarize for a few reasons. First, it contains seventy-four commandments, more than any other Torah portion, and these commandments cover a very broad range of topics. Second, there is not an obvious logic for the order in which Moses shares these commandments with the Jewish people. He seems to jump around randomly from topic to topic.

That said, here are some subjects Moses addresses.

Moses returns to the topic of war, and he gives additional requirements about the treatment of war prisoners. He also stresses the importance of keeping camps clean during time of war to protect the health of soldiers.

There are several commandments that deal with marriage and divorce, including the penalties for a husband who says bad things about his ex-wife after a divorce. Related to the topic of marriage are some commandments regarding children, such as the right of a firstborn son to a double portion of his father's inheritance and the procedure for dealing with a son who is so rebellious and disobedient that the parents are at a loss about what to do.

We find a variety of commandments that seem concerned about public safety and looking out for others. For example, Moses tells the people that they must build a safety fence on a home with a flat roof. He reminds them that they must return a lost object to its owner and that they must help a neighbor when his animal has fallen because of its burden.

There are commandments related to business, like the prohibition against withholding or delaying a worker's wages and the obligation to always have accurate weights and measures. Moses tells the people that they cannot collect interest on any loans they make to other Jews.

Moses discusses things that go beyond business and impact a people's daily lives, like giving charity and mandatory gifts for the poor.

There are commandments that are widely observed to this day, like the obligation to attach fringes to four-cornered garments (tzitzit), as well as commandments that are still discussed and debated, like shooing away a mother bird before taking any eggs from her nest.

Finally, Moses tells the people about two important events that occurred in their past that they must always remember. The first is the story of God punishing Miriam with a skin disease called tzara'at[1] for speaking badly about Moses. The second is Amalek's attack on the Jewish people as they left Egypt. Amalek's goal was to show the nations of the world that the God of the Jews was not all-powerful, and thus, Moses tells the people, God has vowed an eternal war against Amalek.

Life Lessons from *Ki Teitzei*

So many commandments. So many possible life lessons for us to consider, and, of these, there are two, which you'll probably find interesting as they touch upon the issues of animal cruelty and misbehaving children.

Don't Be Cruel

Even if you've never heard of PETA (which stands for People for The Ethical Treatment of Animals), the organization probably

---

1. This Hebrew word is often and incorrectly translated as leprosy. While *tzara'at* is a white infection of the skin, which causes translators to confuse it with leprosy, it is something different. It has no equivalent in post-Biblical times.

affects your life in some way. Founded in 1980, the organization has a simple goal: to protest, loudly and publicly, against cruelty to animals in all its forms.

PETA has done much over the years to make people aware of the mistreatment of animals. It has also helped change the way many of us shop and eat. Today it's impossible to shop in a grocery store and not see items like cage-free eggs or hormone and antibiotic free meat for sale, not to mention all the plant-based meat substitutes (like Beyond Beef and Impossible Burgers) that are now available.

It would be easy to think that this concern for the well-being of animals is something new and unique to modern society. But that would be incorrect. Judaism has always been concerned with the humane treatment of animals, which is why the Torah has many commandments that deal with this issue.[2] For example, the Torah forbids us from cooking a baby goat in its mother's milk.[3] The Torah also prohibits killing a mother animal and her offspring (be it for food purposes or for a sacrifice in the Temple) on the

---

2. We should note that God has always been concerned for the welfare of all His creations, humans and animals alike. Thus, when God gives Noah seven commandments after he and his family leave the ark, He specifically protects animals against unduly cruel slaughter by banning the practice of cutting a limb off a living animal.

3. Exodus 23:19.

same day.[4] And of course, we have in this week's reading the commandment about shooing away the mother bird before taking her eggs. What do these three examples have in common? Each recognizes the bond between animals and their young, whether it involves sheep, goats, cattle, or birds, and each reflects a concern for the emotional pain of the mother, who should not have to see the killing of her young.

These three examples have one other thing in common: they all have something to do with meal preparation. The Torah discusses COOKING a kid in its mother's milk, SLAUGHTERING a cow and its offspring on the same day, and TAKING the chicks or eggs away from the mother bird. Why is this? One answer is that while the Torah gives us permission to eat animals, it also requires that we be sensitive and compassionate in our interactions with animals, even as we prepare to cook and eat them!

Despite these common elements, the Talmudic sages and later rabbinic authorities seem to see in the obligation to shoo away the mother bird an additional lesson. These scholars argue that sending away the mother bird is not about sparing her feelings. Rather, it is a message to us to always be compassionate in our actions and never be cruel.

Let's consider this carefully.

There is no doubt that animals share a bond with their young. Scientists have shown this to be particularly true in certain species like whales, elephants, and great apes. But is this true for all animals? Do other animals feel sad or upset when their young are taken away? We cannot say for sure, but that is not the point. God gave His commandments to humans, not to animals, and they are meant to make us better people. They teach us to be kind and generous and honest. They require us to pursue justice and strive to do the right thing.

Maybe sending away the mother bird spares her some sort of emotional distress. Or maybe she doesn't feel a thing. But by sending her away, we are setting an example for ourselves to be compassionate, even if our compassion is misplaced.

---

4. Leviticus 22:28.

Ki Teitzei Deuteronomy 21:10—25:19

Do you have a pet? If so, is it your job to take care of it? Whether you have one or not, do you think that taking care of a pet can teach you about helping and caring for people, too? Can you think of one example that shows how this can be true?

Ki Tavo

Deuteronomy 26:1—29:8

Summary of This Week's Reading

Our reading begins with Moses telling the people of the commandment to bring their first fruits to the Temple. (We will discuss this commandment in greater detail below.) Moses here adds two important details. First, this commandment only applies to fruits and produce associated with the land of Israel: wheat, barley, dates, figs, grapes, pomegranates, and olives. Second, when people bring their first fruits to the Temple, they must recite a brief thanksgiving prayer to God and then give the fruit as a gift to the priests.

Moses goes on to discuss other gifts Jewish farmers are required to give to the priests and the Levites who also worked in the Temple. He also tells them about special gifts of fruits and grains they are to give to the poor. Some of these gifts were given every year, and some were only given in years three and six of a seven-year cycle.

The remainder of the reading describes how Moses reminds the people that they selected God to be their God and that God, in turn, chose them to be His holy nation. Moses even spells out specific steps the people are to take to reinforce this reminder. For example, he informs the Jews that they are to gather large stones when they cross the Jordan River to enter the land of Canaan. These stones are to be plastered, and the entire Torah is to be engraved upon them. Another set of stones must also to be inscribed with the entire Torah and be set on Mount Ebal.

To further emphasize the importance of remembering their special relationship with God, Moses describes a ceremony that is to take place when the people enter Canaan.

Half the people will go up to Mount Grizzim, and the other half will go up to Mount Ebal. The elders of the Levite Tribe are to gather in between these two mountains, and they bring the Holy Ark with them. When all the people are in place, the ceremony begins.

The Levites and priests face one mountain and then turn to the other. While facing Mount Grizzim, the Levites and the priests utter a blessing, and all the people answer "Amen." They then turn to Mount Ebal and utter a curse that is the opposite of the blessing just recited. The people again answer "Amen."[1]

These curses and blessings are intended to show the people how seriously they are to take the rewards and consequences of observing or ignoring God's commandments.

Life Lessons from *Ki Tavo*

Have you ever heard people talk about "human nature"? It's a term used to describe how humans naturally behave, and it includes characteristics shared by all people. It's often used to explain how people think, feel, and even act, or, as some would put it, it's meant to describe what makes humans "human."

In our reading this week, it's clear that both God and Moses understand human nature. Let's see how this affects the Jewish people as they prepare to enter the land of Canaan.

Knowing Who Contributed What

If you were to ask your classmates which of their accomplishments they are most proud of, you'd certainly get a lot of different answers.

1. For example, the Levites and priests would face Mount Ebal and say, "Blessed be the man that does not make any sculptured or molten image." All the people, on both mountains, would answer "Amen." Then they turn towards Mount Ebal and recite the curse, saying: "Cursed be the man who makes any graven or molten image." All the people, on both mountains, would answer "Amen." And so on, until all the blessings and curses found in this reading have been recited.

Ki Tavo Deuteronomy 26:1—29:8

Maybe they turned in the best book report in the class or came in first in your school's Science Fair. Perhaps it is that their baseball team or soccer team won the championship. Could be they're really good at individual sports like tennis and swimming. Or maybe they've won awards for dance or for playing a musical instrument.

No matter what your friends (or you for that matter) have accomplished, they did not do so on their own. They surely had help from their parents, teachers, coaches, or even their friends. And if they understand this, they were probably quick to thank all those who helped them.

This is exactly the lesson Moses is trying to teach the Jewish people when he gives them the commandment of the first fruits.

After the Jews conquered the land of Canaan, almost everyone was a farmer (even if they had other jobs, too) because families back then grew their own food. Being a farmer is difficult, especially in those times. Farmers often worked alone, and much of their work was done by hand. Plus, many things were beyond their control, like how much rain fell or how hot or cold it was throughout the year. It would make sense that farmers naturally felt a great sense of accomplishment at the end of the harvest season (especially if they had grown enough food to feed their families). The question is, did they recognize or acknowledge the help they got?

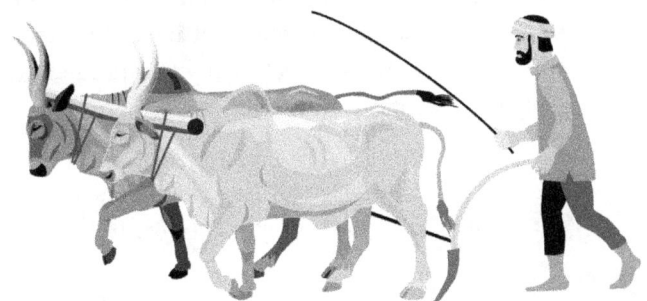

Wait a minute. What help? Didn't we just say that farmers were often on their own?

Yes, we did, but the simple answer is they got help from God, as Moses makes very clear when he commands the people about first fruits. Moses tells the people that they must bring the first fruits or grains of their harvest to the Temple as a thanksgiving offering to God. Moses also gives them very strict instructions about what to say when they bring their first fruits:

> I acknowledge this day before the LORD your God that I have entered the land that the LORD swore to our fathers to assign us. . . . He brought us to this place and gave us this land, a land flowing with milk and honey. Wherefore I now bring the first fruits of the soil which You, O LORD, have given me.[2]

With these words, farmers are forced to think not only about what they accomplished, but how they did so, too. Without enough rain and good soil and proper temperatures, no farmer can succeed. And these things, which seem like normal parts of nature, are gifts from God. (Some rabbis go so far and call them "miracles"!) Once farmers recognize this, they understand that it's appropriate for them to publicly thank Him, not only in the current year, but in each and every year.

It's safe to say that Moses understood human nature and understood the need for this commandment of the first fruits. It is only natural for people to feel proud when they accomplish something important or meaningful. It may be challenging to admit, but the truth is that people rarely accomplish things on their own. Somewhere, somehow, they got help. Admitting this takes nothing away from a person's accomplishments. It instead makes it more likely that they will continue to get help when needed, which in turn will help them continue to be successful.

> *Do you always recognize the help you get, be it with schoolwork or sports or anything else? If so, how do you do this? With a simple "thank you?" By returning the favor?*

Rewards and Consequences

With the commandment of the first fruits, we got a glimpse of Moses's understanding of human nature. There is a second

[2]. Deuteronomy 26:3–10.

example in this week's reading, and it involves the idea of rewards and consequences.

People usually want to do the right thing, and they often do. Just think about what happens when your parents ask you to do something. Of course, you want to do what they ask. It's human nature. They're your parents, and they love you (and you love them, too). But sometimes there are distractions. A video game to play. A favorite television show to watch. A friend to play with. A good book about Deuteronomy to read. And before you know it, you've forgotten (or ignored) what your parents asked you to do.

For the record, it's no different with adults. They want to do what's asked of them or expected of them. But life has so many distractions.

That's why we have rewards and consequences in so many areas of our lives. It's as true today as it was when the Jewish people were in the Sinai wilderness preparing to enter the land of Canaan. God understands that the Jews want to obey His commandments, but He also knows that wanting to do something and actually doing it are not always the same thing. That is why God tells Moses to instruct the people about the blessings and curses we see in this week's reading. These blessings and curses are not so different from the rewards and consequences your parents probably give you when they ask you to do something. Blessings and rewards are meant to motivate us to get things done. Consequences and curses are what happens when we don't do those things.

In a perfect world, we would not need rewards or consequences. Kids would always do what their parents and teachers ask of them. Parents would always do what their bosses and colleagues at work ask of them. But the world is not perfect, and neither are we. God understands that, and the blessings and the curses He instructs Moses to share with the people are His way of motivating us to follow His commandments.

> *Do your parents use rewards and consequences? Which works better for you? Rewards or consequences? Why?*

Nitzavim

Deuteronomy 29:9—30:20

Summary of This Week's Reading

A covenant is a kind of agreement, and in this week's reading, Moses has one final task to complete, sealing the covenant between God and the Jewish people. What do God and the Jewish people agree to in this covenant? The Jews agree to accept God as their God, and God in turn makes the Jews His chosen people.[1] *Moses emphasizes one important detail about this covenant. Namely, that it is not limited to those who were physically present on that day. Rather, it includes all future generations of Jews as well.*

At this point, Moses begins to talk about the future of the Jewish people. He starts by warning the people not to be tempted by the idols of Egypt or of the other nations they have encountered during their wanderings in the Sinai desert. Moses makes very clear the serious consequences that will befall any individual, family, or tribe that abandons the covenant with God. And what will the consequence be if the entire people sin? Exile! They will be kicked out of Israel, the very land God has promised them.

This all sounds scary and depressing. Sensing this, Moses gives the people a reason to be hopeful. Should they be exiled, says Moses,

---

1. Being chosen by God to be His special nation does not mean that the Jews are—or see themselves as being—superior to other nations. Being God's chosen people instead means that the Jews are tasked with teaching the world about the one, true God and with being role models to show humankind's potential for goodness and holiness.

they will eventually turn back to God. God in turn will gather the Jewish people from even the most distant lands and return them to the land of Israel. Once there, the Jewish people will once again serve God and will be blessed in many ways, including large, healthy families, fields that produce large crops, and animals that produce many offspring. What's more, the terrible things that befell the Jewish people when they were exiled to foreign lands will happen to their enemies who made their lives so difficult.

Moses gives the people further encouragement. He urges them to follow God's commandments and tells them that doing so will not be as hard as they might think. He utters these well-known verses:

> It is not in the heavens, that you should say, "Who among us can go up to the heavens and get it for us and impart it to us, that we may observe it?" Neither is it beyond the sea, that you should say, "Who among us can cross to the other side of the sea and get it for us and impart it to us, that we may observe it?" No, the thing is very close to you, in your mouth and in your heart, to observe it.[2]

Moses concludes this speech by telling the Jewish people they have been given the freedom to choose between good and evil and between life and death. Their choices will determine whether or not they will receive God's blessings or curses. So, Moses implores the people to choose wisely and choose good.

Life Lessons from *Nitzavim*

Moses's concluding remarks really summarize this week's reading. It's all about our ability to choose and make decisions for ourselves, from what we'll do to what type of people we can and will become.

It's You Who Decides

The Marvel Cinematic Universe (MCU) seems to be taking over the film industry, and why not? Everyone loves superheroes. And one of the things that makes superheroes and other fictional

---

2. Deuteronomy 30:12–14.

Nitzavim Deuteronomy 29:9—30:20

characters so likable is their core beliefs. You know, those beliefs that define who they are and how they act. Take Spider-Man for example. Uncle Ben taught his nephew that "with great power comes great responsibility," and that principle guides him always, both as Peter Parker and as Spider-Man.

Countries, organizations, and even people can also be said to have core beliefs. Think about the United States. When asked what they know about the United States, one of the first things most people mention is the famous statement from the Declaration of Independence, "we hold these truths to be self-evident, that all men are created equal."

Not surprisingly, religions are defined by their core beliefs, too. To be a Christian, one must believe that Jesus is the Son of God and is equal with God;[3] that Jesus lived a perfect, sinless life;[4] that Jesus was crucified to pay the penalty for the sins of humankind;[5] and that Jesus rose from the dead.[6]

Islam also has its core beliefs. The religious obligations of all Muslims are summed up in the Five Pillars of Islam.[7] These include belief in God (whom they call Allah) and his Prophet

---

3. John 1:1, 49; Luke 22:70; Mark 3:11; Philippians 2:5–11.
4. Hebrews 4:15; John 8:29.
5. Matthew 26:28; 1 Corinthians 15:2–4.
6. Luke 24:46; Mark 16:6.
7. The Five Pillars are alluded to in the Quran, and some are even specifically stated in the Quran, like the Hajj to Mecca.

Muhammad; the obligation to pray five times a day (at dawn, noon, mid-afternoon, sunset, and after dark); the obligation to donate a fixed portion of their income to community members in need; the obligation to make at least one visit to the holy city of Mecca during one's lifetime; and the obligation to fast during the daylight hours of Ramadan, the ninth month of the Islamic calendar.

Judaism, of course, has its core beliefs, but unlike Christianity and Islam, there is no fixed number of core beliefs in Judaism and no definitive list of them either.[8] This is very interesting, because Talmudic rabbis and later sages had no problem with numbering the commandments in the Torah and with compiling detailed lists of these commandments.[9] However, when it comes to core beliefs, these same rabbis and scholars were reluctant to say that a Jew must believe this or must believe that. There are, they say, a handful of beliefs that go to the heart of what it means to be a Jew, but certainly no long list or required "must dos."

That being said, being Jewish means believing that God is unique and the creator of the heavens and Earth. It means believing that God gave His Torah to the Jewish people at Mount Sinai. And it means believing in the concept of free will.

What do we mean by free will? Free will is God's way of saying to us that we decide who we will be and what we will do with our lives. Yes, God gives us commandments to follow, just like a parent tells a child what he or she must do. The goal, both of God and of parents, is to help individuals become better people: more honest, more caring, more attentive to the needs of the world and of others. This is what God wants for us. This is what parents want for their children. But in the end, the responsibility rests with us to choose what type of person we will become.

---

8. The major exception is Maimonides's Thirteen Principles of Faith, which is part of the introduction to his commentary on the tenth chapter of Talmud Sanhedrin.

9. See Shemot Rabbah 33:7, Bamidbar Rabbah 13:15–16; 18:21, and Talmud Yevamot 47b. However, if one were to count every commandment spelled out in the Torah, the number is much greater than 613, which is why this 613 figure is typically understood to represent categories of commandments, not necessarily individual commandments.

Nitzavim Deuteronomy 29:9—30:20

If you find this all a bit confusing, don't worry. It is confusing. It's a little surprising, too. God gives us commandments to follow and then tells us that we really don't have to obey them if we don't want to. What sense does that make?

The best answer is perhaps this. Belief that is forced is not true belief. Not every faith accepts this as true, and over the centuries, countless thousands have been forced to accept certain religions under the threat of violence or at the point of a sword. Judaism rejects this, and Jews believe that God does, too. God seeks those who serve Him by choice and out of love and devotion. Only this type of service can bring a person to a true and lasting relationship with God, which is exactly what our Father in heaven desires.

What types of things do your parents let you choose for yourself? What things aren't you allowed to choose for yourself? How do you feel when you get to choose? How do you feel when you don't get to choose? And when you don't get to choose, why do you think it wasn't a choice in the first place?

You Get to Choose, Too

Free will is truly a gift from God, but it comes with responsibilities. Making choices means being willing to accept the responsibly for our choices. Sometimes, maybe even most of the time, we make good choices, but sometimes we don't. And bad choices can result in wrong or improper actions on our part and on occasion, friends getting hurt.

What happens when we make bad choices and hurt our friends? Several things actually. There is recognizing that we need to make things right and then deciding to take action to do so. Apologies are certainly in order. Replacing a lost item or fixing a broken one can be involved. Doing nice things for the friend we've hurt is another good step. Of course, having a friend who is willing to forgive is a must.

It's no different when it comes to our relationship with God. God has given us commandments He hopes and expects us to follow (because, as we've already discussed, these commandments are intended to help make us better people). Some of these are easy to follow. So we choose to do so. Others can be hard or boring or confusing to us. So we ignore them. Sometimes we understand that certain commandments are really good for us, and still, we make bad choices and decide not to observe them.

It's not accurate to describe God as angry when we make bad choices. Frustrated is a better word. But God is patient, too. He waits for and even urges us to make good choices again. The prophet Zechariah summed this up best when he shared God's message with the Jewish people: "Turn back to me—says the LORD of Hosts—and I will turn back to you"[10]

Moses talks about this process of turning back to God in this week's reading. Here is what he has to say:

> When all these things befall you—the blessing and the curse that I have set before you—and you take them to heart amidst the various nations to which the LORD your God has banished you, and you return to the LORD your God, and you and your children heed His command with all your heart and soul, just as I enjoin upon you this day, then the LORD your God will restore your fortunes and take you back in love. He will bring you together again from all the peoples where the LORD your God has scattered you.[11]

We call what Moses describes here "repentance" (*teshuva* in Hebrew, from the Hebrew word for "to return"). Moses makes clear to the people that God will accept their repentance if it is real and sincere. Building off this assurance, the Talmudic rabbis and later sages spend a lot of time discussing how one can return to God after making bad choices that lead to improper or even sinful behavior.

All agree that the first step in returning to God involves a choice on our part. We can of course choose to keep doing the bad things we've been doing, or we can choose to stop. How do people choose to stop? Part of it is recognizing how bad, harmful, or wrong these actions might be. Arriving at this recognition

---

10. Zechariah 1:3.
11. Deuteronomy 30:1–3.

usually involves feeling bad or embarrassed by what we've done. And the truth is, if we don't feel bad or embarrassed by our actions, we'll never stop doing them.

What comes next? Deciding that we will no longer act in this bad or improper way. And it is not that we won't act that way for a day or a week or a month. It is deciding that we're done with it all together. Then we make one more decision: to start doing the right thing again.

There is one last step: admitting what we've done wrong. Not to ourselves and not in our heads, but saying it out loud. The Jewish prayer ritual on Yom Kippur, the Day of Atonement, is full of confessional prayers that spell out in detail what we've done wrong over the past year. Let's remember that God does not need our confessions. He already knows what we've done (be it good or bad). The confession, this listing of our bad choices and the bad actions that resulted, is for us. It helps us recognize our mistakes, just as it helps make our determination to do right even stronger.

This *teshuva* process is very important to the idea of free will. God gives us choices and lets us decide. He knows we're not perfect. He knows we'll make mistakes. But, as Moses promises in this week's reading, He will always be there for us when we decide to come back to Him.

Are Your Choices Really Yours to Make?

As we noted in the summary of this week's reading, the last task Moses must complete before his death is to arrange a covenant between God and the Jewish people. Moses does this, but says something a little strange in the process:

> I make this covenant, with its sanctions, not with you alone, but both with those who are standing here with us this day before the LORD our God and with those who are not with us here this day.[12]

---

12. Deuteronomy 29:13–14.

Who is Moses referring to when he says, "those who are not with us here this day"? The commonly given answer is future generations of Jews, that is, the grandchildren and great-grandchildren and so on of the people standing before Mount Sinai at that moment. But this seems to go against what we've just learned about free will. Think about it. If we are free to choose what we do or don't do, how can Moses commit future generations to accepting this covenant (which is what he just did!)?

One way to approach this question is to differentiate between the Jewish people and the individuals who make up that people. Perhaps Moses could (and did) commit the people as a whole to observing the covenant in his time and in the future. But that commitment still left individuals with a choice, and understanding this choice involves how we define the word "Jewish."[13]

When individuals say they are Jewish, they might be referring to their religion. In other words, they could mean that they attend a synagogue, that they observe the Sabbath, that they keep kosher, and so on. But Judaism is more than a religion. It is a nationality. Seen from this perspective, when you say, "I am Jewish," it means that you consider yourself part of the Jewish people. It is thus possible for people who have never set foot in a synagogue and who do not believe in God to still see themselves as Jewish.[14] Perhaps you even know such people!

This difference between religion and nationality is important because Moses seems to be committing future generations to being part of the Jewish people. This is not an issue of free will. It is a matter of birth. You are born a Jew, or you're not.[15]

---

13. Two of the major denominations of Judaism in America today—Orthodox and Conservative—require that one's mother be Jewish for a person to be considered Jewish. The other denominations—Reform and Reconstructionist—say that it is sufficient if either parent is Jewish.

14. Jews living in Israel prove the point. According to a 2016 Pew Research Study, nearly half of Israeli Jews (49 percent) are not ritually observant.

15. While Judaism does not actively seek converts, Jewish law is quite clear that converts have the same status as those who are born Jewish. Additionally, Jewish law requires that converts are warmly welcomed into all aspects of Jewish life and that we should not ever remind them of their past lives and actions prior to becoming Jewish.

If that's the case, what is Moses's goal here when it comes to future generations?

Over the centuries, many, many Jews decided that they no longer wanted to be Jewish. Sometimes they simply hid the fact that they were Jewish and lived their lives like their non-Jewish neighbors. Sometimes they converted to other religions. But history has shown us that the nations of the world do not easily allow Jews to deny their Jewishness. When these nations passed laws banning Jews from certain professions or from owning land or from even living in these countries, their rulers did not ask, "Jew, do you attend synagogue on Saturdays? Jew, do you eat pork or not?" Their laws simply applied to those they saw as Jews. Depending on where and when you lived, it was enough to have a Jewish parent (or even a grandparent) to be labeled as a Jew.

Moses must have anticipated this. He knew that God had granted the Jewish people free will, and so Moses could not "force" future generations to follow God's commandments. But he could commit those who came after him to being part of the Jewish people. It is as if he were saying to us that we cannot drop out of the Jewish nation. It is as if Moses is challenging each of us to define our Jewishness for ourselves and not let the nations of the world define for us what it means to be a Jew.

There is a second way in which Moses's committing future generations to observing the covenant is related to the issue of free will. With this commitment, Moses seems to recognize that the actions and decisions of those who came before us impact how we act and think and guide us in making choices.

In modern times, this issue of how big an affect our parents and grandparents have on us is framed as one of "nature versus nurture." In simple terms, all living things (people included) have inherited qualities they have no control over, like the color of their eyes or how tall they'll grow to be. Many believe how you act can also be an inherited trait. For example, if you have a bad temper or if you cry easily at the movies, it's because your parents are the same way. This is what we mean by "nature." But there are events or experiences in all our lives which also shape how we act, and these we describe as "nurture."

When Moses makes a commitment for future generations, he is hinting to us that "nurture" will always be part of our lives. Future generations will learn from what their ancestors did and accomplished, and this will affect how these future generations make decisions. If one of your parents was a teacher or a first responder or a banker or a graphic designer and you decide to also do that when you grow up, the choice will still be yours. But your choice will be influenced by how happy or successful your parent was in their chosen profession.

No matter how we look at it, Moses deciding on behalf of future generations (meaning us!), does not in any way limit our free will. Instead, it forces us to think even more deeply about the choices we make, especially with respect to our Jewish identities.

> Here is an experiment for you to do with your parents. Make a list of the ways you think you are just like your parents and a second list of how you're different from your parents. Then ask your parents to make the same lists about their parents. When you're finished, compare your lists. Can you find things you think you "inherited" from your parents? From your grandparents? What does this tell you about "nature versus nurture"?

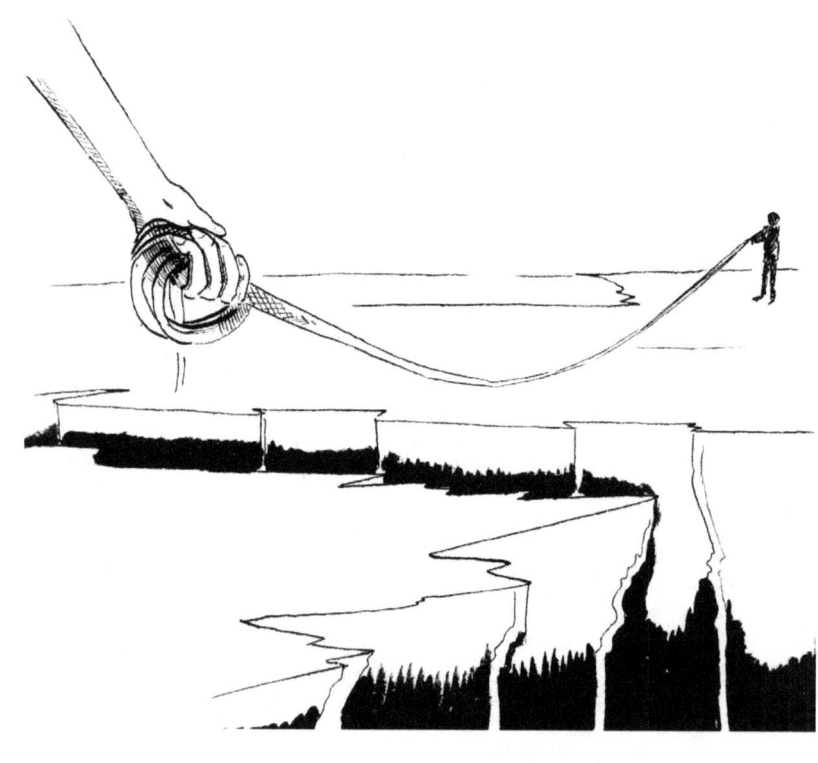

Vayelech

Deuteronomy 31:1–30

Summary of This Week's Reading

The end is really here for Moses. He reminds the people that he turns 120 years on this very day and that he is not permitted to cross the Jordan River with them. Instead, Joshua will lead them, and God will go before them and destroy their enemies in Canaan, just as He did with the Emorites and Bashanites. This is why, says Moses, the people should be strong and not fear their enemies.

Moses summons Joshua and tells him that he, too, should be strong and courageous because God will be with him as he leads the Jewish people and will not abandon him. Moses then writes the entire Torah onto scrolls and gives one scroll to the priests and one to each of the tribal leaders.

Next on Moses's "to do" list: explain the commandment of Hakhel, which is a special gathering of all the Jewish people (men, women, and children) that is to take place every seven years during the holiday of Sukkot (Tabernacles) following the Sabbatical year. At this assembly, the king will publicly read certain sections of the Torah.

God commands Moses to enter the Mishkan together with Joshua. God appears to them both with a warning. A time will come when the Jewish people abandon God, and many bad things will befall them as a result. To prepare for this, God tells Moses to write a "song" and teach it to the people. (This song appears in next week's reading.) *This song is meant to warn the Jewish people of the consequences of turning away from God.*

After he leaves the Mishkan, Moses takes one of the Torah scrolls he wrote and gives it to the Levites. He tells them to place it beside the Ark which holds the tablets God gave to Moses at Mount Sinai. Moses then gathers the entire nation to hear the song. In it, he calls upon the heavens and earth to be witnesses that the Jewish people were warned about the terrible things that will happen when they turn away from God.

Life Lessons from *Vayelech*

Moses spends a lot of time in this week's reading thinking about the future of the Jewish people. His words can give us some guidance for thinking about our own futures, too.

Safeguarding Your Legacy

Legacy is a word you may have heard but don't know what it means. And even if you do know what it means, perhaps you haven't given it much thought.

A legacy is the impact a person has on his or her family, friends, and community long after they're gone. It's true that for some a legacy involves money, be it money left to their children or to a favorite charity. But the concept of a legacy goes beyond monetary gifts. As one author put it: "It is about the richness of the individual's life, including what that person accomplished and the impact he or she had on people and places. Ultimately, the story of a person's life reflects the individual's legacy."[1]

Young people typically don't think about their legacies. That's not surprising, as they have their whole lives ahead of them. But as they grow older and build families of their own, many people ask

---

1. Mary Gormandy White, "What Is a Person's Legacy?", *Love to Know*, https://dying.lovetoknow.com/about-obituaries-memorials/what-is-persons-legacy.

themselves questions like, what impact did I have on my children? What will I be remembered for after I'm gone?

It's clear from this week's reading that Moses has thought a lot about his legacy. He has already asked God to appoint a good leader to take his place. This God does when He selects Joshua. Both Moses and Joshua are described in various places in the Bible as *Eved Hashem* ("servant of God"). Taking note of this, the Talmudic rabbis say that Moses is like the sun and Joshua like the moon.[2] They point out that moon's role is to reflect the sun's light at night when the sun does not shine. For these rabbis, Joshua's defining feature was like that of the moon, meaning, he reflected Moses's leadership and continued Moses's legacy.

Teaching God's law to the people, as he had done for forty years in the wilderness, was another big part of Moses's legacy. To protect this, Moses wrote copies of God's Torah for each of the tribes, and he even put a copy in the Ark that sat in the center of the *Mishkan*. He also made sure that Joshua and the elders were well versed in God's laws and could thus continue teaching them to the Jewish people.[3]

The fact that the Jewish people continue to thrive and grow to this day is a testament of Moses's legacy! What can we learn from this?

Moses did not make plans for preserving his legacy until late in his life. But he lived his whole life in a way that made leaving a legacy easy. He literally influenced and touched the lives of hundreds of thousands of people. Most of us will not have such a large impact. But we can live each day with an eye to the future. We can and should ask ourselves often, are my actions having a positive impact on the people around me? Am I doing things I can be proud of not only today, but in ten or twenty years from now?

---

2. Bava Batra 75a.

3. This process begun by Moses of training scholars to teach God's laws to the next generation continued for centuries, as described in the first Mishnah of the Talmudic tractate Avot: "Moses received the Torah at Sinai and transmitted it to Joshua, Joshua to the elders, and the elders to the prophets, and the prophets to the Men of the Great Assembly."

A Curious Student's Guide to the Book of Deuteronomy

If you live your life in such a way, building a legacy won't be hard. It may not be as big as Moses's, but it can be every bit as everlasting for your family and friends.

Who is your favorite person from the Bible? What is his/her legacy?

Safeguarding Connections

Ask any parent how they would feel if all their grown children lived in the same city as they did, and a smile would likely cross their lips. Of course, parents want their children and grandchildren to live near them. But this has become the exception rather than the rule. Kids go away to college, and maybe they move back home. Maybe they don't. Or maybe they meet their future partner at college, and that person lives in another town and wants to be close to their family.

With iPhones and FaceTime and texting and Zoom, it is easier than ever for families to keep in touch. But electronic communications are not the same as spending time in person with those you love and are closest to.

VAYELECH Deuteronomy 31:1–30

Moses seems to have foreseen the challenges of staying connected with people who live far from you. He also understood how important it was for all the Jewish people to maintain a connection with one another. True, ancient Israel was a small country (just as it is today), but in those times, it could take a lot of time and effort to travel distances that today seem very short. Given this, how could the Jewish people stay connected?

Part of the answer can be found in the commandment of *Hakhel*. Here's how it works:

> In ancient Israel, every seventh year was a *Shemitah* year. For an entire year, farmers and those people who worked with them were to set aside their work and devote the year to Torah study. Their focus was to be on their spiritual, rather than their physical needs.[4]

At the beginning of the eighth year (which was the first in the new seven-year cycle), the people were ready to return to their fields and orchards. But before they could, on the second day of the holiday of Sukkot (which was sixteen days into the new year), all the people—men, women, and children alike—were to gather in Jerusalem. There, they would thank God for His assistance during the *Shemitah* year. They would hear the king publicly read portions of the Torah. As Moses describes it in this week's reading:

> Gather the people—men, women, children, and the strangers in your communities—that they may hear and so learn to revere the LORD your God and to observe faithfully every word of this Teaching.[5]

---

4. The Sabbatical year was among the most challenging commandments in the Torah. It took great faith not to farm for a whole year when farming was your only source of food. Sadly, the commandment was ignored far more often than it was observed. According to the Talmudic sages the Sabbatical year was ignored seventy times during the days of the first temple. In their view, this explains why the exile to Babylonia after the temple's destruction lasted seventy years. It was as if God were giving the land a chance to "catch up" on the Sabbatical years it lost.

5. Deuteronomy 31:12.

Hakhel was a way for the people to strengthen their connection to God, but it was also a way for the nation to reconnect. The Sukkot holiday lasted for a week, and immediately after it was a special one-day festival call Shemini Atzeret. These days were a time to worship and offer sacrifices to God, but they were also filled with much joy and many festive meals. In fact, Sukkot was so festive that the Talmud rarely refers to it by its formal name, but instead uses the term "the Holiday." (The Hebrew word for holiday [*chag*] is one associated with great joy and festivity!)

Moses probably could not have imagined how hectic life would become today. Long workdays for parents. Busy school days followed by after school activities for kids. Phones continually ringing or pinging constantly demanding your time and attention. Even when parents and grown children live in the same city, they cannot always find the time to get together. But, as we see in the commandment of *Hakhel*, Moses foresaw a need for families and communities to spend what we now call "quality time" together.

This is an important lesson to be learned from *Hakhel*. Our goal, however, should be to make these connections more often than every seven years.

> *When your weeks get very busy, how do you and your parents stay connected? What about your friends? What other things could you be doing?*

Haazinu

Deuteronomy 32:1–52

Summary of This Week's Reading

Most of this week's Torah reading is the poetic song mentioned in last week's reading. The song is a prophecy of what will happen to the Jews—both good and bad—until the end of times. Moses warns the people that God will punish them harshly if they turn away from Him (which they ultimately did, resulting in the destruction of both the first and second temple). But Moses assures the people that, in the end, God will turn His anger against their enemies. At that time, when God avenges the sufferings of the Jewish people, the nations of the world will sing the praises of Israel. With this, the song of Haazinu concludes.

Moses, with the help of Joshua, teaches this song to the people, and he shares with them his final request: "Take to heart all the words with which I have warned you this day. Enjoin them upon your children, that they may observe faithfully all the terms of this Teaching."[1] It is at this point that God tells Moses to climb up Mount Nebo, from where he can see the land of Israel before he passes away.

Life Lessons from *Haazinu*

In last week's reading, God tells Moses to write a "song" and teach it to the Jewish people. Moses shares that song in this week's

---

1. Deuteronomy 32:46.

reading. The song is filled with beautiful imagery and metaphors, as we see in this verse: "May my discourse come down as the rain, My speech distill as the dew, Like showers on young growth, Like droplets on the grass." Such imagery can make it difficult to understand the song and difficult to find life lessons in it. That's why we will examine the role songs like this play in the Bible and how they are relevant to our lives today.

When Thank You Doesn't Feel Quite Enough

People have different reasons for thanking God. Maybe it's for something miraculous and wonderful, like your parents winning a million-dollar lottery. Maybe it's for a relative or friend recovering from a serious illness. Maybe it's for something as simple as getting a good grade on a math test. People feel a need and a desire to thank God for any number of reasons, but one thing we can agree on is that thanking God should be a part of our lives.

Jewish law adds an interesting twist to the idea of thanking God. The Talmudic sages put it this way: "One is obligated to recite a blessing for the bad just as he recites a blessing for the good, as it is stated: 'And you shall love the Lord your God with all your heart.'"[2]

Perhaps you're wondering, how does the commandment to love God with "all your heart" teach us that we must bless God over evil, just as we bless Him over good? The answer is found in the unusual Hebrew spelling in this phrase of the word "your

---

2. M. *Brachot* 9:5. The second part of the quote is from Deuteronomy 6:5.

heart." This word is typically written in Hebrew with a single "bet" (ב), but here it is written with two "bets" (לְבָבְךָ). The rabbis see these two bets as hinting that one must worship God with both of one's impulses—the good impulse and the evil impulse—which also means that one blesses God for good and bad alike.

What an interesting perspective. Jewish law states that we are to thank God for bad things that happen to us just as we thank Him for the good He does for us. Thanking God for the bad and the good is another way of recognizing that God is involved in every aspect of our lives, whether we see it or not.[3] And this sense of obligation of thanking God is reflected in almost every page of a Jewish prayer book (*siddur* in Hebrew).

It is not surprising that the prayers we recite daily and on Shabbat are full of thanks to God, but this might make you wonder, are the words of the prayer book the only way we can thank God? What a great question, and one answer is found in Moses's song that makes up this week's reading.

The Hebrew word used to describe Moses's song is *shira*. Interestingly, in modern Hebrew, there's a difference between *shir*, which means a song, and *shira*, which means a poem. In the Bible, there is no difference, which means songs like that of Moses are a mixture of song and poetry. More importantly, wherever we find a *shira* in the Bible, its author uses it to both praise and thank God for some miraculous event, as can be seen in the table below.

---

3. Jewish law does not expect people to react in the same way to bad news as they do to good news. To illustrate this point, consider the case of Rabbi Mordechai Dov Twersky of Hornistopol, Ukraine. Rabbi Twersky once suffered a terrible loss: a great fire burned down his home as well as his study hall, which was filled with many valuable manuscripts. At first, he was greatly depressed, but then he remembered that one must bless over the bad as well as the good. He thus pushed aside his depression and suddenly seemed joyful. His students were confused and asked him about his change of attitude. Rabbi Twersky answered as follows: "While we are commanded to bless, we are not commanded to ignore. We may wonder why God sends such difficulties our way, but once we realize that it is His will, we offer a blessing even for the disasters and difficulties we experience." https://www.jpost.com/jewish-world/judaism/world-of-the-sages-blessings-for-the-bad.

Book	Name	Circumstance
Exodus 15:1–19	*Shirat HaYam*	Splitting the Sea of Reeds after the Exodus from Egypt
Deuteronomy 32:1–43	*Shirat Ha'azinu*	The end of forty years in the Sinai wilderness
Joshua 12:1–24	*Shirat Yehoshua*	The defeat of the thirty-one kings
Judges 5:1–31	*Shirat Devorah*	The complete conquest of Northern Israel
2 Samuel 22:1–51	*Shirat David*	Establishing the monarchy of David

Looking at this table, we see that the first *shira* sung in Jewish history occurred after the Jews emerged unharmed after crossing the Sea of Reeds while Pharoah's soldiers and chariots were all destroyed when the sea returned to its natural state. This was indeed a great miracle, one that called for much praise and thanks to God. But as we think about this particular *shira*, we should pause for a moment and ask another important question. If *shira* was an important way to thank God, and the midrash says that the song sung at the Sea of Reeds was especially dear to Him,[4] why was there no *shira* before this one?

The midrash struggles with this question. It teaches that from the beginning of time, God was waiting for someone to sing *shira*. He gave Adam the greatest gift possible, the gift of life, but Adam didn't sing *shira*. God did many great and wondrous things for Abraham, like saving him from Pharoah[5] and aiding him in the war against the four kings,[6] but Abraham didn't sing *shira*. God did great things for Isaac, too, like helping him in his struggles with Abimelech[7] and making him very wealthy,[8] but Isaac didn't sing

4. Midrash Rabba 24:4.
5. Genesis 12:10–20.
6. Genesis 14:1–16.
7. Genesis 26.
8. Genesis 26:12–13.

shira. God saved Jacob from Esau's hatred and Laban's deceit, but Jacob didn't sing *shira*. Only at the Sea of Reeds was *shira* sung, and this, claims the midrash, made God very, very happy.

Adam, Abraham, Isaac, and Jacob may not have sung *shira*, but they certainly were grateful for the goodness God showed them. They offered thanks to God with prayer and with sacrifices. Why was that not enough? What made the *shira* sung by the Jews after the splitting of the sea so special (something we can ask about each *shira* listed in the table above as well)?

Two things come to mind.

First, the stories we read in Genesis, from Adam to Jacob, are primarily about individuals. These individuals had special and perhaps unique relationships with God, and God in turn did many marvelous things for these people and their families. But there was not yet a Jewish people to interact with God.

Second, the help that these individuals received from God (for which they were very grateful) happened naturally or could be explained logically. Were the armies of the four kings greater in number than Abraham and his servants? Most definitely, but small armies throughout history have often defeated larger armies. Isaac's fields and flocks were more productive than those of his neighbors, 100 times more productive according to the verses in Genesis. Did this require a miracle? No. It could be explained by better soil, healthier animals, and workers who were more skilled and worked harder. Jacob was known as a person of incredible honesty.[9] Could such an honest person outsmart someone so skilled with lies and deceit as Laban? He could, and he did!

All this explains why the Genesis personalities did not sing *shira*. God helped them as individuals, whereas at the splitting of the sea, God saved the entire Jewish people. And this was true each time we find a *shira* in the Bible.

There's more. The help God gave the Jewish people that inspired them to sing *shira* was supernatural, like splitting the sea or feeding the Jews manna from heaven during their forty years

---

9. Jacob is known in the rabbinic tradition as a pillar of truth, as it states in the book of Micah 7:20, "give truth to Jacob."

in the wilderness. The kind of normal, day-to-day help God gave the people in Genesis was deserving of thanks. But *shira* seems to be reserved for the miraculous. Why? Because the nature of the miracle inspired the people to offer a different and higher level of praise and thanksgiving.

What does all this mean for us who are living at a time in which there are no obvious and open miracles?

Thanking others for the help they give us, be it friends, family, or God, is always an appropriate and correct thing to do. A simple "thank you" is generally enough for your friends and family. For God, the prayers of praise and thanks we offer on weekdays and the Sabbath are likely sufficient. Must you do something more? Can you do something more? That's up to you. Flowers and cards can be nice, and as for God, there are special blessings of thanks for special occasions, like when we eat a new fruit or get a new shirt or sweater.

Flowers, cards, special blessings, these are nice ways to give thanks, but they are things you are giving, not things you made or wrote on your own. Maybe that's the lesson we can draw from *shira*. It shows us that we can create our own ways of thanking others and thanking God when we think the normal way does not adequately show what we're feeling. For us, it's not a question of miracles being performed or of the whole nation being saved. It's really a matter of how deep our sense of gratitude is. Feeling so grateful that you "burst out in song" would be a wonderful experience, for you and God both.

> We can't send God cards or flowers, so how exactly can we show Him gratitude? How do you show Him gratitude? What if you tried this? The next time you want to show thanks, try bursting out in prayer to the heavens! God may be smiling even more than you will be!

V'Zot HaBeracha

Deuteronomy 33:1—34:12

Summary of This Week's Reading

Shortly before he passes away, Moses blesses each of the twelve tribes, beginning with the descendants of Leah. Moses blesses the tribe of Reuben with life in this world and the next and Judah with success and victory in his battles[1]

Next comes Levi. Moses praises this tribe as the only one to remain faithful to God through the many difficulties the Jewish people faced in their long journey through the wilderness.

Moses then turns to the descendants of Rachel. He gives Benjamin the title of "God's beloved." Because of the tribe's lofty status, the temple will ultimately be built in its portion of Israel. Moses then

---

1. Given that Moses begins his blessings with the descendants of Leah and follows the birth order of her sons, Simeon's blessing should have followed that of Reuben. Yet, as scholars and sages alike have noted, Moses does not include the tribe of Simeon in his blessings, and they wonder why. One commonly given answer is this: Simeon is omitted because its members were most prominent in the sinful behavior involving the worship of the idol Baal Peor. (Numbers 25:1–3) How do we know this? Just look at the large decrease in its numbers in the census taken after the incident of Baal Peor. Plus, their tribal leader was a leader of those who turned to idol worship and was killed by Phineas. (Numbers 25:6–8) Another answer often cited is that Moses followed Jacob's example. Jacob did not directly bless Simeon or Levi, and Moses thought to do the same thing. However, because Aaron had been chosen by God Himself to be the High Priest and the tribe of Levi to serve as priests in the *Mishkan*, Moses simply could not exclude Levi from his blessings.

declares that Joseph's portion in the land of Israel will be blessed with plentiful rain, dew, and produce. He also blesses Joseph with unusual ox-like strength which he will use to defeat his enemies.

Moses returns to Leah's descendants. He blesses Zebulun with success in his business endeavors and Issachar in his Torah studies.

Now come the descendants of the handmaidens, Bilhah and Zilpah.

Moses blesses Gad with the strength of a lion—who tears off the arm and head of his enemy with one blow—and an expanding portion in Israel. He also praises Gad for choosing a portion on the eastern bank of the Jordan River and for leading the troops in battle in the conquest of Canaan.

Dan's blessing echoes that of Gad, as Moses blesses him with the strength of a lion cub. Naftali's portion in Israel is that he is praised as one filled with God's blessing. Moses concludes his blessings of the tribes with Asher, whom he blesses with sons and with an abundance of olive oil, so much that he will dip his feet in oil.

In addition to blessing the individual tribes, Moses praises the Jewish people as a whole. He notes that God is always ready to come to their assistance. "O happy Israel! Who is like you, A people delivered by God, Your protecting Shield, your Sword triumphant!"[2]

We now reach the end of the Torah. As God instructed him, Moses goes up to the top of Mount Nebo where God shows him all the land of Israel. According to the Midrash, God then kisses Moses who dies at the age of 120, with his eyes never dimmed and his skin never dried. God Himself tends to Moses's burial. His exact burial place is a mystery to this day. Joshua becomes the leader upon Moses's death, but there is little celebration, as the people mourn Moses for thirty days.

The Torah's concluding words praise Moses, telling us that he was the greatest prophet to ever live and that he performed incredible and awesome miracles before the eyes of all of Israel.

---

2. Deuteronomy 34:29.

V'Zot HaBeracha Deuteronomy 33:1—34:12

Life Lessons from *V'Zot HaBeracha*

We see in the Torah several instances of fathers blessing their children before their deaths. The story of Isaac wishing to bless his sons and of Jacob pretending to be his brother Esau at his mother's urging is arguably the best-known example. But Jacob blessing his twelve sons is more significant, and it seems to have served as a model for Moses blessing each of the twelve tribes before his death.

Much has been written about these blessings. The Midrash (Bereshit Rabbah 100:13) goes so far as to suggest that Moses's blessings are a natural continuation of the blessings of Jacob:

> "And this is" (*v'zot* in Hebrew) what their father spoke unto them.³ A man like me is destined to bless you, and, from the very place where I [Jacob] concluded—from there will he begin. At the moment, Moses our teacher rose to bless them, he began with "and this is the blessing" (*v'zot haberacha* in Hebrew)—from the very place where their father concluded. This then is the meaning of the expression *v'zot* what their father spoke unto them.⁴ [Their father Jacob told them that the next blessing they receive would be from a man who will begin with *v'zot*— *v'zot haberacha*].

A closer look at the similarities and differences between these two sets of blessings will help us learn some valuable life lessons.

Unity is Key

Thinking about Jacob's life, it would not have been surprising had he not blessed some of his sons. Let's start with his eldest son Reuben.

As we read in the book of Genesis, Jacob's life was not easy, and having two sisters, Rachel and Leah, as wives was challenging at times.⁵ Like Sarah before her, Rachel gave her handmaiden Bilhah to her husband when she was unable to have children. Leah

---

3. Genesis 49:28.
4. Genesis 49:28.
5. See, for example, Genesis 30:14–16.

already had given birth to four sons by this point, but she thought (mistakenly as it turns out) that she would have no more, and so she gave her handmaiden Zilpah to Jacob as a wife.[6]

Having four wives was complicated, and while Rachel was Jacob's most beloved wife, he spent private time as he wished with all four women. When Rachel died giving birth to Benjamin, Reuben assumed that his father would spend most of his private time with his mother Leah. This was not the case. Jacob spent more time with Bilhah. It is unclear why. Maybe she reminded him of Rachel. Maybe she was already helping to raise Benjamin's older brother Joseph and was better able to help with the new baby. Whatever the reason, Reuben thought this was disrespectful to his mother, and so, according to rabbinic tradition, he moved his father's bed from Bilhah's tent to Leah's tent. Jacob was understandably very angry. How dare his son interfere in such private matters?

Now consider the case of Simeon and Levi.

After their sister Dinah was kidnapped by Shechem, Jacob and his sons were desperate to save her. Jacob thought he could rescue her by making a deal with Shechem and his father Hamor. The deal seemed simple enough. Jacob's sons would marry women from Shechem's city, and Shechem and his friends would marry women from Jacob's family. They would thus become one big happy family. There was just one precondition. All the men from Shechem's city would first have to circumcise themselves. This was not an easy thing to do, because circumcision for adults is very painful. But Shechem was so determined to marry Dinah that he convinced everyone to go through with this.

There was just one problem: Simeon and Levi. They were too angry about how their sister had been treated, and they were not willing to make the deal. So, they pretended to go along and waited for Shechem and the other men to be circumcised. Once this was done, and after these men were too weak to fight back, Simeon and

---

6. Jewish tradition states that Rachel and Leah both knew that Jacob was destined to have twelve sons. Thus, when Leah thought she had stopped having children, she gave Zilpah to Jacob as a wife in the hope that Zilpah's children would help the family grow to twelve sons. It should be noted that Bilhah and Zilpah were secondary wives, just as Hagar was a secondary wife to Sarah.

V'Zot HaBeracha Deuteronomy 33:1—34:12

Levi snuck into their city and killed everyone! Jacob was furious, because he was convinced that Simeon and Levi's reckless behavior put their entire family at risk.[7]

And how can we forget that the brothers sold Joseph into slavery and then tricked their father into believing that Joseph had been killed by a wild animal?[8] Did Jacob ever learn the truth about how Joseph became a slave? Rabbis and scholars have debated this question for years. But even those who say Jacob never really knew think he must have had his suspicions.[9]

Despite all this, Jacob blesses each of his twelve sons. He may not have completely forgotten the past actions of his sons,[10] but Jacob saw each of them as having a role to play in the family. Jacob seems to understand that family members sometimes have disagreements and that sometimes family members do hurtful things to one another. But by blessing all twelve of his sons, Jacob

---

7. Genesis 34:30.

8. Genesis 37:31-33.

9. Chapter fifty of Genesis gives us a hint that Jacob knew the truth. The text there tells us that after Jacob's death, the brothers feared that Joseph would seek revenge (50:15-22). To protect themselves, the brothers told Joseph that Jacob had specifically instructed them to ask Joseph to forgive "the offense and guilt of your brothers who treated you so harshly." Nowhere in the text do we find Jacob saying such a thing, and in fact, many rabbis and scholars insist he would never have said such a thing. Why? Because, as they argue, Jacob felt that Joseph was above taking revenge. And Jacob could only think Joseph was above taking revenge if he had a reason to take revenge. Why would Jacob think Joseph had a reason for taking revenge? Jacob must have known the truth about Joseph becoming a slave!

10. The language Jacob uses in his blessings shows us that he may have forgiven but has certainly not forgotten these actions. To Reuben he says: "Unstable as water, you shall excel no longer; For when you mounted your father's bed, You brought disgrace—my couch he mounted!" (Genesis 49:4) To Simeon and Levi he says: "Simeon and Levi are a pair; Their weapons are tools of lawlessness. Let not my person be included in their council, Let not my being be counted in their assembly. For when angry they slay a man, And when pleased they maim an ox. Cursed be their anger so fierce, And their wrath so relentless. I will divide them in Jacob, Scatter them in Israel." (Genesis 49:5-7)

demonstrates to his children and grandchildren (and to us, too!) the importance of family unity.[11]

Like Jacob, Moses would also seem to have reasons not to bless some or all of the people.

At the sea, before God performs a great miracle and divides it so the Jews can safely cross it, the people question Moses's leadership. They yell at him: "Was it for want of graves in Egypt that you brought us to die in the wilderness? What have you done to us, taking us out of Egypt?"[12] Even though God miraculously provides the people with manna every day for forty years, the Jews again turn against Moses and verbally attack him: "If only we had died by the hand of God in the land of Egypt, when we sat by the fleshpots, when we ate our fill of bread! For you have brought us out into this wilderness to starve this whole congregation to death."[13]

---

11. In our times, people sometimes refer to the importance of family unity with the expression "blood is thicker than water." This means that our family bonds are always more important than any other relationship, even ones we make by choice.

12. Exodus 14:11.

13. Exodus 16:3.

At other times, the people did more than attack Moses with their words. They acted inappropriately or sinfully.

When a small band of individuals (3,000 according to the rabbinic tradition) worshipped the golden calf, the rest of the people stood by silently, doing nothing to prevent this outrageous behavior.

When the spies returned from scouting out the land and delivered a false report, only Joshua and Caleb protested. Everyone else spent that night crying in their tents and feeling sorry for themselves![14]

When Korah questioned Moses's leadership and led a rebellion against him, the tribe of Reuben sided with Korah against Moses.

When the Jewish people were at Shittim (after Balaam tried but failed to curse the Jewish people), many men allowed themselves to be seduced by the women of Moab into acting inappropriately with them and worshipping their idols. One man even had the nerve to do such inappropriate things right in front of Moses and the other leaders of the Jewish people![15]

More than once during their stay in the Sinai wilderness, God grew so frustrated with the Jewish people that He threatened to destroy them and start anew with Moses. In each instance, Moses defended the people and begged God to forgive them. It should thus come as no surprise that he, too, forgave them and blessed each of the tribes. Moses knew that while unity is very important to a family, without it, a people cannot exist.

> *Does your family have any routines or rituals you turn to when you're not getting along with one another? Do these work to help bring you all back together again? Why do you think these work? Which ones seem to help the most?*

Focusing on the Present Versus the Future

Of all the differences between the blessings of Jacob and Moses, the most important one may involve time. How so? In his

---

14. Numbers 14:1.
15. Numbers 25:6.

blessings, Jacob shares his thoughts on his sons in the present and then shares his hopes for them in the future, whereas Moses seems only focused on the present. Let's see if we can figure out why this is and what we can learn from this.

One factor which explains the difference between these two sets of blessings is the different relationships Jacob and Moses have with those being blessed. Jacob is their father, and understandably his blessings focus on his relationship with his sons. As a father, he knows that each of his sons deserves his attention. Moses, however, is a leader of, not the father of the people. It is thus logical that his focus is on the nation as a whole, not any particular group of individuals. Want proof of this? Take a close look at his blessings—how he begins them and ends them—and you will see that Moses is truly focused on the people as a nation, one in which their current division into twelve tribes will become increasingly less important.

Now we can better understand why the tone of their blessings is so different.

From the very beginning, Jacob indicates to his sons that he will not only share with them insights about who they are now, grown men, in the prime of their lives, but that he will also prophesize future events. Moses the leader may hint to future events in his blessing, but his main focus is on the tribes as they are in the present, not in the future.

This makes a great deal of sense.

Parents are very involved in their children's lives and also in the lives of their grandchildren (and maybe even great-grandchildren, too). Parents look to the future, because in most instances they are helping to shape and build the future of their family. Not so with a leader. The influence of even the greatest leaders, like a Washington or a Lincoln or a Moses, ends when they leave office or certainly with their deaths. Moses gets this, and this is why he focuses on the here and now. He is essentially telling the people: "I have been with you for forty years. I have brought you to this point. I know what you are capable of. But the rest is up to you. Only you can make your future."

V'Zot HaBeracha Deuteronomy 33:1—34:12

This is not to say that people forget or ignore their leaders once they are gone. Historians to this today look to the presidencies of Washington and Lincoln when discussing the type of country America can and should be. And Jews to this day follow the teachings of Moses, so much so that certain Jewish laws are described as "laws given to Moses at Sinai."

On a practical level, what does this all mean for us?

Even as children, we realize the importance of our parents and the impact they will have on our lives. No one can or will shape us as people like our parents do. But others do have an impact on us: grandparents, aunts and uncles, maybe even our siblings and cousins. Then there are teachers and mentors. Ask your parents about this, and they are likely to start by telling you about their parents, but it's just as likely that they will include a favorite teacher[16] or someone who helped them with their career or chosen profession.

Just because Moses did not dwell on the future in his blessing to the Jewish people does not mean he was not an important part of that future.

---

16. I know this to be true from personal experience. Over the years I have spoken with a number of my former students who tell me that they still remember what I taught them in fourth grade and how much those lessons still matter to them as adults.

Postscript

At its core, the book of Deuteronomy is all about the future. Over and over in his farewell speech, Moses reminds the Jewish people of mistakes they made during their forty years in the wilderness. He does this not to make them feel bad, but to help them learn from their mistakes so they avoid repeating them in the future. He often warns them of the consequences in the future should they turn away from God. And his final blessings to the people are meant to inspire them to be their best selves in the future.

This also is true for my Curious Student's Guide series. These books are very much about the future. I didn't realize this until I was near the end of this fourth and final installment in the series, but I should have from the very onset of this endeavor.

The idea for writing these books came from my oldest daughter. A few years ago, she and her family moved back to Atlanta, where my wife and I, along with her two siblings, live. Her oldest son, our first grandchild, was then four years old. Like the good Jewish educator I am, I bought him a gift upon his arrival in Atlanta: a collection of parasha books. I had done a lot of research and bought what I thought was the best one on the market at that time. Not long thereafter, my daughter called me and told me that she thought the books I had purchased were "terrible." (My daughter is not one to mince words.) She then told me that I should write a series of parasha books for my grandson.

Postscript

Is there anything more future-oriented than writing books for a grandchild?

I took my daughter's challenge to heart. I knew I didn't want to create picture books on the weekly parasha, which would have been most appropriate for a four-year-old, but which was, quite frankly, something I was not up to. I thought long and hard about what I hoped my grandson would learn about each week's parasha and how it would likely be taught to him when he got to elementary school. I realized that I wanted him to learn more about the weekly readings than answers to trivia questions. How many days of creation were there? How many days and nights did the rains fall when Noah was in the ark? How many angels came to visit Abraham? How many wells did Isaac dig? How many years was Jacob away from his father when he was forced to live with Laban?

I think you get the point.

This, of course, led me to think in terms of life lessons I wanted my grandson to learn from each parasha, and these life lessons (and the questions we ask that help us discover life lessons in each week's reading) became the heart of these books. My hope was (and still is) that my grandson (as well as the young students who read these books either on their own or with their parents) will take these lessons to heart, that they would help him start thinking about the person he wanted to be and could be.

Perhaps you're asking (after all, you are a curious student, are you not?), can lessons we learn as children really stick with us and really shape us as we grow into adults? After spending twenty years teaching students of various ages, I know the answer is yes. And if you ask your parents if they think this is true, I believe they will likely say yes as well.

Robert Fulghum, an American author known for his short essays, summed it up best in his book *All I Really Need to Know I Learned in Kindergarten*. His list of lessons learned in kindergarten that stuck with him for life include things like:

Postscript

> Share everything.
> Play fair.
> Don't hit people.
> Put things back where you found them.
> Clean up your own mess.
> Don't take things that aren't yours.
> Say you're sorry when you hurt somebody.

These may strike you as things only kids would be concerned with, but trust me, adults should follow these simple rules as well. Fulghum also included a few things that seem more grownup, like:

> Live a balanced life—learn some and think some and draw and paint and sing and dance and play and work every day some.
> Be aware of wonder.
> Goldfish and hamsters and white mice and even the little seed in the Styrofoam cup—they all die. So do we.
> And then remember the Dick and Jane books and the first word you learned—the biggest word of all—LOOK.

The point is this. Real life lessons—meaningful life lessons—can and do have an impact on you, no matter how old you are when you learn them! And this, I have come to realize as I finish the last of these books, is why the Curious Student's Guide series is all about the future.

It is my most sincere hope that the life lessons found in my books made sense to you, that you read them and thought to yourself, "I can do that! I should do that!" If that's the case, maybe these lessons helped you do things differently and maybe be a better person. And if you are somehow a little different or a little better today, you will carry this forward as you grow into the person you can and perhaps should be.

I want to leave you with one last life lesson. It's one that Moses hints at throughout his farewell speech and one I think is best summed up in a beautiful sentiment from a poem entitled "Andrea del Sarto" by Robert Browning: "Ah, but a man's reach should exceed his grasp, Or what's a heaven for?"

Postscript

Browning, and Moses before him, is telling us to think big, to dream big. Will you discover a cure for cancer? Become president of the United States? Invent the next life-changing technology? Who knows? But by striving for greatness, even if you fall a little short, you will live a full and rich life. And in doing so, you will gather life lessons you'll be able to pass along to your children and grandchildren.

About the Author

Rabbi Reuven Travis earned his bachelor's degree from Dartmouth College, where he graduated Phi Beta Kappa, with a double major in French literature and political science. He holds a master's degree in teaching from Mercer University and also earned a master's in Judaic studies from Spertus College. He received his rabbinic ordination from Rabbi Michael J. Broyde, dean of the Atlanta Torah MiTzion Kollel, after spending four years studying with Rabbi Broyde and the members of the kollel.

Rabbi Travis worked in Jewish day schools for twenty years and taught students from second grade through high school. He has previously published three scholarly works on the books of Job, Numbers, and Genesis, respectively, and is currently working on a number of new book projects. He also teaches online classes on topics ranging from the Bible to Jewish medical ethics to American history.

www.ingramcontent.com/pod-product-compliance
Lightning Source LLC
Chambersburg PA
CBHW071443160426
43195CB00013B/2016